![GAO Accountability·Integrity·Reliability]

Highlights

Highlights of GAO-05-866, a report to the Ranking Minority Member, Subcommittee on Oversight of Government Management, Committee on Homeland Security and Governmental Affairs, U.S. Senate

August 2005

DATA MINING

Agencies Have Taken Key Steps to Protect Privacy in Selected Efforts, but Significant Compliance Issues Remain

Why GAO Did This Study

Data mining—a technique for extracting knowledge from large volumes of data—is being used increasingly by the government and by the private sector. Many federal data mining efforts involve the use of personal information, which can originate from government sources as well as private sector organizations.

The federal government's increased use of data mining since the terrorist attacks of September 11, 2001, has raised public and congressional concerns. As a result, GAO was asked to describe the characteristics of five federal data mining efforts and to determine whether agencies are providing adequate privacy and security protection for the information systems used in the efforts and for individuals potentially affected by these data mining efforts.

What GAO Recommends

GAO is making recommendations to the agencies responsible for the five data mining efforts to ensure that their efforts include adequate privacy and security protections. The agencies responsible for the five efforts we reviewed generally agreed with the majority of our recommendations, but disagreed with others.

www.gao.gov/cgi-bin/getrpt?GAO-05-866.

To view the full product, including the scope and methodology, click on the link above. For more information, contact Linda D. Koontz (202) 512-6240 or koontzl@gao.gov.

What GAO Found

The five data mining efforts we reviewed are used by federal agencies to fulfill a variety of purposes and use various information sources, including both information collected on behalf of the agency and information originally collected by other agencies and commercial sources. Although the systems differed, the general process each used was basically the same. Each system incorporates data input, data analysis, and results output (see figure).

The Data Mining Process

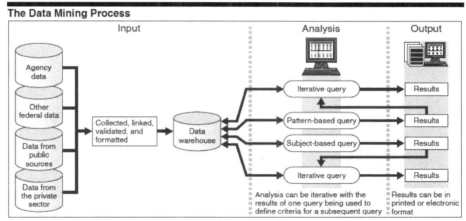

Source: GAO, adapted from Vipin Kumar and Mohammed J. Zaki.

While the agencies responsible for these five efforts took many of the key steps required by federal law and executive branch guidance for the protection of personal information, they did not comply with all related laws and guidance. Specifically, most agencies notified the general public that they were collecting and using personal information and provided opportunities for individuals to review personal information when required by the Privacy Act. However, agencies are also required to provide notice to individual respondents explaining why the information is being collected; two agencies provided this notice, one did not provide it, and two claimed an allowable exemption from this requirement because the systems were used for law enforcement. In addition, agency compliance with key security requirements was inconsistent. Finally, three of the five agencies completed privacy impact assessments—important for analyzing the privacy implications of a system or data collection—but none of the assessments fully complied with Office of Management and Budget guidance. Until agencies fully comply with these requirements, they lack assurance that individual privacy rights are being appropriately protected.

United States Government Accountability Office
Washington, D.C. 20548

August 15, 2005

The Honorable Daniel K. Akaka
Ranking Minority Member
Subcommittee on Oversight of Government Management
Committee on Homeland Security and Governmental Affairs
United States Senate

Dear Senator Akaka:

Data mining—a technique for extracting knowledge from large volumes of data—is being used increasingly by the government and by the private sector. Many federal data mining efforts involve the use of personal information, which can originate from government sources as well as private sector organizations.[1]

This report responds to your request that we review federal data mining efforts that use personal information. Specifically, our objectives were to describe the characteristics of selected federal data mining efforts, including each system's data sources, outputs, and uses, and to determine whether agencies are providing adequate privacy and security protections for the information systems used in these efforts and for individuals potentially affected by them.

To address these objectives, we reviewed five data mining efforts at the Small Business Administration (SBA), the Department of Agriculture's Risk Management Agency (RMA), the Department of the Treasury's Internal Revenue Service (IRS), the Department of State (State), and the Department of Justice's Federal Bureau of Investigation (FBI). These efforts were selected for review because they met several criteria, including the use of personal information and data obtained from another agency or a private sector source, and because they were used for one of

---

[1]For purposes of this report, we define "personal information" consistent with the Privacy Act's definition of a "record," which includes all information associated with an individual and includes both identifying information and nonidentifying information. Identifying information, which can be used to locate or identify an individual, includes name, aliases, Social Security number, e-mail address, driver's license identification number, and agency-assigned case number. In this report, we refer to identifying personal information as personal identifiers. Nonidentifying personal information includes age, education, finances, criminal history, physical attributes, and gender.

several specific purposes.[2] To address both objectives, we reviewed agency-provided documents and interviewed agency officials. To evaluate the agencies' implementation of key privacy protections, we also reviewed related notices, reports, and other documents. Our scope and methodology are discussed in more detail in appendix I.

We performed our work from May 2004 to June 2005 in accordance with generally accepted government auditing standards.

Results in Brief

The data mining efforts we reviewed have a variety of purposes and uses and employ different data inputs and outputs. In addition to information collected directly from individuals, the efforts use information provided by other agencies (such as the National Oceanic and Atmospheric Administration) and private sector sources (such as credit card companies). These efforts include the following:

- The RMA effort is used to detect fraud, waste, and abuse in the Federal Crop Insurance Program.

- The Citibank Custom Reporting System, an offering of the General Service Administration's Government-wide Purchase Card program, is used by State to analyze government charge card spending patterns by its employees.

- The data mining effort of the FBI Foreign Terrorist Tracking Task Force helps federal law enforcement and intelligence agencies locate foreign terrorists and their supporters in the United States.

- The IRS's Reveal system is used to detect evidence of financial crimes, fraud, and terrorist activity.

- The SBA Lender/Loan Monitoring System, provided under contract by Dun & Bradstreet, is designed to identify, measure, and manage risk in two SBA loan programs.

---

[2]We selected efforts that were intended to meet at least one of the following purposes: improving service or performance; detecting fraud, waste, and abuse; detecting criminal activities or patterns; or analyzing intelligence and detecting terrorist activities.

While the agencies responsible for these five efforts took many of the key steps required by federal law and executive branch guidance for the protection of personal information, none followed all key procedures. Specifically, most agencies notified the general public that they were collecting and using personal information and provided opportunities for individuals to review personal information, when required by the Privacy Act. However, agencies are also required to provide notice to individual respondents explaining why information is being collected: two agencies provided this notice, one did not provide it, and two claimed an allowable exemption from this requirement because the systems were used for law enforcement. Agencies' compliance with key security requirements that are intended to protect the confidentiality and integrity of personal information was inconsistent. Finally, three of the five agencies had prepared a privacy impact assessment—an important tool for analyzing the privacy implications of a system or data collection—of their data mining efforts, but none of the assessments fully complied with Office of Management and Budget (OMB) guidance. Until agencies fully comply with these requirements, they lack assurance that individual privacy rights are appropriately protected.

We are making recommendations to the agencies responsible for the five data mining efforts to ensure that their efforts include adequate privacy and security protections.

In providing comments on a draft of this report, the agencies generally agreed with the majority of our recommendations, but disagreed with others. USDA agreed with the majority of our recommendations, and stated that it plans to take the necessary steps to address them. The General Service Administration's (GSA) Assistant Commissioner for Acquisition (who provided comments via e-mail) generally disagreed with our recommendations, stating that the Privacy Act does not apply to its system and that it had taken appropriate security measures. However, in our view, GSA's system is subject to the Privacy Act. Additionally, while we acknowledge GSA's efforts to secure its system, it is nonetheless required to comply with the specific requirements of the Federal Information Security Management Act of 2002 and with related guidance. State and SBA generally agreed with our recommendations and provided information on their planned actions. Treasury generally agreed with the recommendation to conduct a new privacy impact assessment, but in response to our recommendation on security, Treasury stated that it believes it already has adequate security measures in place. We acknowledge that while Treasury has applied several security measures, required regular testing and evaluation was not yet in place and we have clarified our recommendation to reflect this. Justice stated that it had no comments on our draft.

Background

In our May 2004 report on federal data mining efforts,[3] we defined data mining as the application of database technology and techniques—such as statistical analysis and modeling—to uncover hidden patterns and subtle relationships in data and to infer rules that allow for the prediction of future results. We based this definition on the most commonly used terms found in a survey of the technical literature. For the purposes of this report, we are using the same definition.

Data mining has been used successfully for a number of years in the private and public sectors in a broad range of applications. In the private sector, these applications include customer relationship management, market research, retail and supply chain analysis, medical analysis and diagnostics, financial analysis, and fraud detection. In the government, data mining was initially used to detect financial fraud and abuse. For example, we used data mining techniques in our prior reviews of federal government purchase and credit card programs.[4]

Following the terrorist attacks of September 11, 2001, data mining has been used increasingly as a tool to help detect terrorist threats through the collection and analysis of public and private sector data. Its use has also expanded to other purposes. In our May 2004 report,[5] we identified several uses of federal data mining efforts. The most common were

- improving service or performance;

- detecting fraud, waste, and abuse;

- analyzing scientific and research information;

---

[3]GAO, *Data Mining: Federal Efforts Cover a Wide Range of Uses*, GAO-04-548 (Washington, D.C.: May 4, 2004).

[4]For more information on the uses of data mining in GAO audits, see GAO, *Data Mining: Results and Challenges for Government Programs, Audits, and Investigations*, GAO-03-591T (Washington, D.C.: Mar. 25, 2003).

[5]GAO-04-548.

- managing human resources;

- detecting criminal activities or patterns; and

- analyzing intelligence and detecting terrorist activities.

While the characteristics of each data mining effort can vary greatly, data mining generally incorporates three processes: data input, data analysis, and results output. In data input, data are collected in a central data warehouse, validated, and formatted for use in data mining. In the data analysis phase, data are typically searched through a query. The two most common types of queries are pattern-based queries and subject-based queries.

- Pattern-based queries search for data elements that match or depart from a predetermined pattern (e.g., unusual claim patterns in an insurance program).

- Subject-based queries search for any available information on a predetermined subject using a specific identifier. This could be personal information such as an individual identifier (e.g., a Social Security number or the name of a person) or the identifier of a specific thing. For example, the Navy uses subject-based data mining to identify trends in the failure rate of parts used in its ships.

The data analysis phase can be iterative, with the results of one query being used to define criteria for a subsequent query. The output phase can produce results in printed or electronic format. These reports can be accessed by agency personnel, and can also be shared with other personnel from other agencies. Figure 1 depicts a generic data mining process.

Figure 1: An Overview of the Data Mining Process

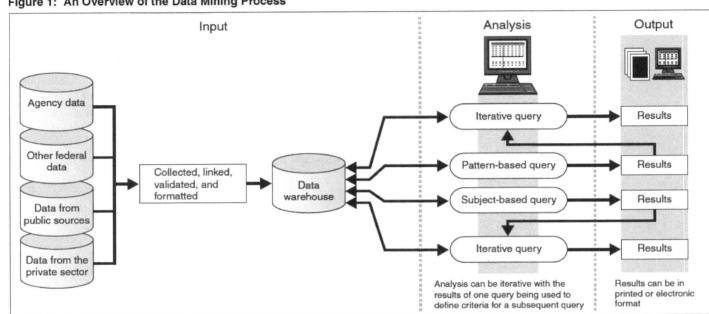

Source: GAO, adapted from Vipin Kumar and Mohammed J. Zaki.

Note: From Vipin Kumar and Mohammed J. Zaki, *High Performance Data Mining, University of Minnesota, undated*; http://www.cs.rpi.edu/~zaki?PSKDDTUT00.pdf.

Data Mining Poses Privacy Challenge

The impact of computer systems on the ability of organizations to protect personal information was recognized as early as 1973, when a federal advisory committee on automated personal data systems observed that "The computer enables organizations to enlarge their data processing capacity substantially, while greatly facilitating access to recorded data, both within organizations and across boundaries that separate them." In addition, the committee concluded that "The net effect of computerization is that it is becoming much easier for record-keeping systems to affect people than for people to affect record-keeping systems."[6]

---

[6]U.S. Department of Health, Education, and Welfare, *Records, Computers and the Rights of Citizens*, Report of the Secretary's Advisory Committee on Automated Personal Data Systems (July 1973).

More recently, the federal government's increased use of data mining has raised public and congressional concerns. A December 2003 report by a task force on information sharing and analysis in homeland security noted that agencies at all levels of government are now interested in collecting and mining large amounts of data from commercial sources.[7] The report noted that agencies may use such data not only for investigations of specific individuals, but also to perform large-scale data analysis and pattern discovery in order to discern potential terrorist activity by unknown individuals.

As we noted in our May 2004 report, mining government and private databases containing personal information creates a range of privacy concerns. Through data mining, agencies can quickly and efficiently obtain information on individuals or groups by exploiting large databases containing personal information aggregated from public and private records. Information can be developed about a specific individual or a group of individuals whose behavior or characteristics fit a specific pattern. The ease with which organizations can use automated systems to gather and analyze large amounts of previously isolated information raises concerns about the impact on personal privacy. Before data aggregation and data mining came into use, personal information contained in paper records stored at widely dispersed locations, such as courthouses or other government offices, was relatively difficult to gather and analyze.

Federal Laws and Guidance Define Steps to Protect Privacy of Personal Information

The 1973 federal advisory committee recommended that the federal government adopt a set of fair information practices to address what it termed a poor level of protection afforded to privacy under contemporary law. These practices formed the basis of the main federal privacy law, the Privacy Act of 1974.

The Privacy Act places limitations on agencies' collection, disclosure, and use of personal information maintained in systems of records. The act describes "records" as any item, collection, or grouping of information about an individual that is maintained by an agency and contains his name or another personal identifier. It also describes systems of records as a group of records under the control of any agency from which information is

---

[7]Markle Foundation, *Creating a Trusted Network for Homeland Security* (New York: December 2003). http://www.markletaskforce.org/Report2_Full_Report.pdf (downloaded Mar. 28, 2005).

retrieved by the name of the individual or by an individual identifier.[8] The Privacy Act requires that when agencies establish or make changes to a system of records, they must notify the public by a notice in the *Federal Register* identifying the type of data collected, the types of individuals that information is collected about, the intended routine uses of the data, and procedures that individuals can use to review personal information.

The Federal Information Security Management Act of 2002 (FISMA) also addresses the protection of personal information. FISMA defines federal requirements for securing information and information systems that support federal agency operations and assets; it requires agencies to develop agencywide information security programs that extend to contractors and other providers of federal data and systems.[9] Under FISMA, information security includes protecting information and information systems from unauthorized access, use, disclosure, disruption, modification, or destruction, including controls for confidentiality—that is, those controls necessary to preserve authorized restrictions on access and disclosure to protect personal privacy.

A third federal law with provisions related to privacy, the E-Government Act of 2002, provides additional protection for personal information in government information systems or information collections by requiring that agencies conduct privacy impact assessments.[10] A privacy impact assessment is

"an analysis of how information is handled: (i) to ensure handling conforms to applicable legal, regulatory, and policy requirements regarding privacy; (ii) to determine the risks and effects of collecting, maintaining, and disseminating information in identifiable form in an electronic information system; and (iii) to examine and evaluate protections and alternative processes for handling information to mitigate potential privacy risks."[11]

Agencies must conduct a privacy assessment (1) before developing or procuring information technology that collects, maintains, or disseminates

---

[8] 5 U.S.C. § 552a (a)(5).

[9] Federal Information Security Management Act of 2002, Title III, E-Government Act of 2002, Pub. L. No. 107-347 (Dec. 17, 2002).

[10] E-Government Act of 2002, Pub. L. No. 107-347 (Dec. 17, 2002), sec. 208.

[11] Office of Management and Budget, Memorandum M-03-22, *Guidance for Implementing the Privacy Provisions of the E-Government Act of 2002* (Washington, D.C.: Sept. 26, 2003).

information that is in a personally identifiable form or (2) before initiating any new electronic data collections containing personal information on 10 or more individuals. Among other actions that should require a privacy assessment, according to guidance from OMB, is significant merging of information in databases, for example, in a linking that "may aggregate data in ways that create privacy concerns not previously at issue" or "when agencies systematically incorporate into existing information systems databases of information in identifiable form purchased or obtained from commercial or public sources."

These laws, along with OMB guidance that outlines how agencies are to comply with the laws, lay out a series of steps that agencies should take to protect the privacy of personal information. Each of the steps includes detailed procedures agencies are to follow to fully implement the requirements. Table 1 lists the key steps, with examples of the procedures agencies are to use to address the step, and the primary statutory source for the protections.

Table 1: Key Steps Agencies Are Required to Take to Protect Privacy, with Examples of Related Detailed Procedures and Sources

Key steps to protect privacy of personal information	Examples of procedures	Primary statutory source
Publish notice in the *Federal Register* when creating or modifying system of records	• Specify the routine uses for the system • Identify the individual responsible for the system • Outline procedures individuals can use to gain access to their records	• Privacy Act
Provide individuals with access to their records	• Permit individuals to review records about themselves • Permit individuals to request corrections to their records	• Privacy Act
Notify individuals of the purpose and authority for the requested information when it is collected	• Notify individuals of the authority that authorized the agency to collect the information • Notify individuals of the principal purposes for which the information is to be used	• Privacy Act
Implement guidance on system security and data quality	• Perform a risk assessment to determine the information system vulnerabilities, identify threats, and develop countermeasures to those threats • Have the system certified and accredited by management • Ensure the accuracy, relevance, timeliness, and completeness of information	• FISMA • Privacy Act
Conduct a privacy impact assessment	• Describe and analyze how information is secured • Describe and analyze intended use of information • Have assessment reviewed by chief information officer or equivalent • Make assessment publicly available, if practicable	• E-Government Act

Source: GAO analysis of the Privacy Act, E-Government Act, FISMA, and related guidance.

Agencies Are Allowed to Claim Exemptions from Some Privacy Provisions

While the federal laws and guidance previously outlined provide a wide range of privacy protections, agencies are allowed to claim exemptions from some of these provisions if the records are used for certain purposes. For example, records compiled for criminal law enforcement purposes can be exempt from a number of provisions of the Privacy Act, including the requirement to notify individuals of the purposes and uses of the information at the time of collection and the requirement to ensure the accuracy, relevance, timeliness, and completeness of records. A broader category of investigative records compiled for criminal or civil law enforcement purposes can also be exempted from a somewhat smaller number of Privacy Act provisions, including the requirement to provide individuals with access to their records and to inform the public of the categories of sources of records. In general, the exemptions for law enforcement purposes are intended to prevent the disclosure of information collected as part of an ongoing investigation that could impair the investigation or allow those under investigation to change their behavior or take other actions to escape prosecution.

The Privacy Act allows, but does not require, agencies to claim an exemption for certain designated purposes. If the agency decides to claim an exemption, the act requires the agencies to do so through a rule that provides the reason behind its decision. Table 2 shows provisions of the Privacy Act from which systems of records used for law enforcement may be exempt.

Table 2: Examples of Privacy Act Provisions from Which Systems of Records Used in Law Enforcement May Be Exempt

Provision	Law enforcement exemptions in the Privacy Act	
	Information used for criminal law enforcement	Information used in law enforcement investigations
Providing individuals with access to their information and the ability to request corrections	Can be exempt	Can be exempt
Notifying individuals of the purposes and uses of the information at the time of collection	Can be exempt	Not exempt
Maintaining records with the necessary accuracy, relevance, timeliness, and completeness	Can be exempt	Not exempt

Source: GAO analysis of federal laws and guidance.

Similarly, the requirement to conduct a privacy impact assessment does not apply to all systems. For example, no assessment is required when the information collected relates to internal government operations, the information has been previously assessed under an evaluation similar to a privacy impact assessment, or when privacy issues are unchanged. Nonetheless, OMB encourages agencies to conduct privacy impact assessments on systems that contain personal information in identifiable form about government personnel, when appropriate. In addition, individual agencies have adopted policies that require assessments for all systems, including those used for government operations.

In June 2003, we reported on our assessment of agencies' compliance with the Privacy Act and related OMB guidance.[12] At that time, we determined that the agencies' compliance was high in many areas, but uneven across the federal government. Agency officials attributed the areas of noncompliance in part to a need for more leadership and guidance from OMB. In our report, we recommended that the Director, OMB, take a number of steps aimed at improving agencies' compliance with the Privacy Act, including overseeing and monitoring agencies' actions, assessing the need for additional guidance to agencies, and raising agency awareness of the importance of the act. In response, OMB established an Interagency Privacy Committee to discuss privacy issues and issued updated guidance. However, it has not addressed our other recommendations: to work with agencies to ensure that they address the areas of noncompliance we identified; institute a governmentwide effort to determine the level of resources needed to fully implement the Privacy Act; and develop a plan to address identified gaps in resources devoted to protecting privacy.

Data Mining Efforts Have a Variety of Characteristics

The data mining efforts that we reviewed have a variety of purposes, uses, and outputs. For example, the efforts are used for program management, law enforcement, and analyzing intelligence. The efforts fulfill these purposes through a mix of subject-based and pattern-based queries, as previously defined, and result in reports that are used by program officials or shared with others. A detailed summary of each of the efforts we reviewed is included in appendixes II through VI. A short summary of the purpose and characteristics of each of the efforts is included here.

---

[12]GAO, *Privacy Act: OMB Leadership Needed to Improve Agency Compliance*, GAO-03-304 (Washington, D.C.: June 30, 2003).

- The purpose of *RMA's data mining effort* is to detect fraud, waste, and abuse in the federal crop insurance program. It is used to identify potential abusers, improve program policies and guidance, and improve program performance and data quality. RMA uses information collected from insurance applicants as well as from insurance agents and claims adjusters. It produces several types of outputs, including lists of names of individuals whose behavior matches patterns of anomalous behavior, which are provided to program investigators and sometimes insurance agencies. It also produces programmatic information, such as how a procedural change in the federal crop insurance program's policy manual would impact the overall effectiveness of the program, and information on data quality and program performance, both of which are used by program managers.

- The purpose of the *Citibank Custom Reporting System* used by State is to detect fraud, waste, and abuse by its employees who use the government purchase card program. The purchase card program is a governmentwide program run by the General Services Administration (GSA). Agencies like State use GSA's master contract to provide their employees with charge cards from an approved vendor. Citibank, the vendor chosen by State, provides its customers with a custom reporting system, which includes several tools that can be used for managing card accounts. State uses the system to analyze government charge card spending patterns by its employees. System outputs include summaries of card account holder information and purchases and can include personal information. Summaries are used by program managers and are on occasion provided to interested parties such as such as State's inspector general, GAO, and OMB for oversight.

- The purpose of *IRS's Reveal* system is to detect criminal activities or patterns, analyze intelligence, and detect terrorist activities. IRS uses the system to identify financial crime, including individual and corporate tax fraud, and terrorist activity. Its outputs include reports containing names, Social Security numbers, addresses, and other personal information of individuals suspected of financial crime, including individual and corporate tax fraud and terrorist activity. Reports are shared with IRS field office personnel, who conduct investigations based on the report's results.

- The purpose of the data mining effort used by the *FBI's Foreign Terrorist Tracking Task Force* is to detect criminal or terrorist activities or patterns and to analyze intelligence. The effort uses two information systems—one classified and one unclassified—to support ongoing investigations by law enforcement agencies and the intelligence community, including locating foreign terrorists and their supporters who are in or have visited the United States. Its outputs include reports based on a request received from field investigators. Reports range from lists of individuals who might meet a certain profile to detailed information on a certain suspect and typically contain personal information. Reports are shared with field investigators, field offices, and other federal investigators.

- The purpose of *SBA's Lender/Loan Monitoring System* is to improve service or performance. The system was developed by Dun & Bradstreet under contract to SBA. SBA uses the system to identify, measure, and manage risk in two of its business loan programs. Its outputs include reports that identify the total amount of loans outstanding for a particular lender and estimate the likelihood of loans becoming delinquent in the future based on predefined patterns.

These systems use information that the agency collects directly, as well as information provided by other agencies, such as the Social Security Administration, and private sector sources, such as credit card companies. Table 3 details the inputs of each effort we reviewed and summarizes each effort by the types of information sources used.

Table 3: Characteristics of Information Inputs Used by the Data Mining Efforts We Reviewed

Data mining effort	Types of inputs: Government — Systems of records	Government — Not identified as systems of records	Commercial sources	Public records	International records
RMA's data mining effort	4 sources, including insurance records on policyholders, agents, and loss adjusters	3 sources: soils data, weather data, and land survey data	None	Various sources, including publicly available information	None
Citibank Custom Reporting System (State)	None	Account information from State employees provided to Citibank	Commercial data provided by Citibank consisting of information on purchases made by State employees	None	None
Reveal (IRS)	4 sources, including suspicious activity reports and extracts of corporate and taxpayer information	None	None	None	None
Foreign Terrorist Tracking Task Force (FBI)	29 sources, including information from FBI's criminal database, immigration and visa data, and customs data	1 source	11 sources, consisting of data from commercial sources	None	4 sources, including lost property reported to Interpol and intelligence data
Loan/Lender Monitoring System (SBA)	1 source, including loan and lender information for SBA's loan programs	None	3 sources, including corporate- and consumer-level data from private companies	None	None

Source: GAO analysis of agency information.

Agencies Addressed Many Required Privacy Provisions, but None Addressed All Requirements

While the agencies responsible for the five data mining efforts took many of the key steps needed to protect the privacy and security of personal information used in the efforts, none followed all the key procedures. Most of the agencies provided a general public notice about the collection and use of the personal information used in their data mining efforts. However, fewer followed other required steps, such as notifying individuals about the intended uses of their personal information when it was collected or ensuring the security and accuracy of the information used in their data mining efforts. In addition, three of the five agencies completed a privacy impact assessment of their data mining efforts, but none of the assessments fully complied with OMB guidance. Complete assessments are a tool agencies can use to identify areas of noncompliance with federal privacy laws, evaluate risks arising from electronic collection and maintenance of information about individuals, and evaluate protections or alternative processes needed to mitigate the risks identified. Agencies that do not take all the steps required to protect the privacy of personal information limit the ability of individuals to participate in decisions that affect them, as required by law, and risk the improper exposure or alteration of their personal information.

Agencies Generally Provided Public Notice as Required

The Privacy Act requires agencies to notify the public, through notices published in the *Federal Register*, when they create or modify a system of records. The act's provisions include requirements for agencies to provide general notice about the operation and uses of a system of records. According to OMB's guidance on implementing the act, this public notice provision is central to one of the act's basic objectives: fostering agency accountability through a system of public scrutiny. This echoes the 1973 federal advisory committee's statement that public involvement is essential for an effective consideration of the pros and cons of establishing a personal data system.

Of the five efforts we reviewed, the personal information used in four (IRS, RMA, FBI, and SBA) were the subject of published system of records notices in the *Federal Register*. The public was not notified in the case of the fifth system—State. Table 4 details the steps agencies took to notify the public about the five efforts we reviewed.

Table 4: Questions Related to Agency Actions to Notify the Public about New or Changed Information Collections or Efforts

Question	Yes	Partial	No	Exempt
Was a timely system of records notice published in the *Federal Register*?	CDE	A[a]	B	
Did the notice indicate the name and location of the system of records?	ACDE		B	
Did the notice specify the category of individuals in the system of records?	ACDE		B	
Did the notice specify the category of records in the system of records?	ACDE		B	
Did the notice specify the routine uses of the system of records?	ACDE		B	
Did the notice specify how the agency stores, maintains, and accesses the records?	ACDE		B	
Did the notice identify the individual responsible for maintaining the information in the system of records and give instructions on how to contact that person?	ACD	E	B	
Did the notice specify the process by which an individual can request notification if the system contains records pertaining to him or her?		E	B	ACD
Did the notice specify the procedures by which an individual can gain access to a record pertaining to him or her and challenge its contents?		E	B	ACD
Did the notice specify the categories of information sources used by the system?	DE		B	AC

Legend:

A: RMA's data mining effort

B: State's Citibank Custom Reporting System

C: IRS's Reveal effort

D: FBI's Foreign Terrorist Tracking Task Force effort

E: SBA's Lender/Loan Monitoring System

Source: GAO analysis of agency information.

[a]RMA's notice was not timely because it was published after its effort had been implemented.

The published system of records notices related to the data mining efforts at IRS, FBI, and RMA generally included the information required by the Privacy Act. However, the notice published by SBA was only partially compliant with the act because it did not clearly describe the process individuals could use to review their information. For example, SBA's notice listed several dozen contacts and indicated that individuals should identify the appropriate contact from the list when making requests related to their information. However, the notice did not describe how to identify which contact would be appropriate.

No notice was published for the Citibank purchase card management tool used by State. As the agency responsible for the governmentwide purchase card program, GSA is responsible for ensuring that the program follows statutory requirements, including those in the Privacy Act. However, it has not published a system of records notice that would cover the activities of State or other agencies participating in the program. According to GSA officials, the agency did not consider purchase card records to be a system of records because it believed the names and addresses it collects pertain to government employees and thus are exempt from the Privacy Act. The GSA officials added that a programwide system of records notice has been partially drafted, but it has not been finalized because it is waiting for guidance from OMB on a recent change to the program that could require the collection of additional personal information. Without adequate notice of this information collection effort, the ability of State employees and the public to participate in decisions about the collection and use of personal information, as envisioned under the Privacy Act, is limited.

IRS, RMA, and FBI did not include in their notices a description of how individuals can review their personal information because they claimed the exemption available for records used in law enforcement.[13]

Two Agencies Allowed Individuals to Access their Information; Others Were Exempt

The Privacy Act requires agencies to, among other things, allow individuals to (1) review their records (meaning any information pertaining to them that is contained in the system of records), (2) request a copy of their record or information from the system of records, and (3) request corrections in their information. Such provisions can provide a strong incentive for agencies to correct any identified errors.

State and SBA provided mechanisms by which individuals could review the information the agencies collected and used in their data mining efforts; the three other agencies claimed allowable exemptions from this requirement. Table 5 details the steps the agencies took to provide

---

[13]The agency rules claiming exemptions from designated provisions of the Privacy Act are published in the Code of Federal Regulations at 7 CFR §1.123 (RMA), 28 CFR §16.96 (FBI), and 31 CFR §1.36 (IRS).

individuals with access to their personal information used in the data mining efforts.

Table 5: Questions Related to Agency Actions to Provide Individuals with Access to Their Personal Records

Question	Yes	Partial	No	Exempt
Does the agency permit individuals to review the records about themselves and have a copy?	BE			ACD
Does the agency permit individuals to request amendments of records pertaining to them?	BE			ACD
Does the agency permit individuals to request corrections to any portion of records pertaining to them?	BE			ACD

Legend:

A: RMA's data mining effort

B: State's Citibank Custom Reporting System

C: IRS's Reveal effort

D: FBI's Foreign Terrorist Tracking Task Force effort

E: SBA's Lender/Loan Monitoring System

Source: GAO analysis of agency information.

Citibank provides State cardholders with monthly statements detailing their purchase card activity and account information—the personal information used in the data mining effort—that cardholders are required to review. State also has a process with Citibank to dispute and resolve any inaccuracies in this information.

SBA's system of records notice described a general procedure that individuals could use to review personal information SBA collects (which is one of the information sources used in the data mining effort.)[14] In addition, the agency has procedures that detail how individuals are permitted to review records relating to them and request amendment.

FBI, IRS, and RMA claimed an allowable exemption for their efforts because their records are used in law or tax enforcement. FBI and IRS have adopted procedures under which they could waive the exemption and

---

[14]As indicated in table 3, SBA's effort also uses information provided by commercial sources. However, the commercial information provided to SBA does not include personal information on individuals.

allow individuals to access their information in cases where disclosure would not endanger ongoing investigations or reveal investigative methods.

Three Agencies Fulfilled or Partially Fulfilled Requirements Regarding the Notification of Individuals When Personal Information Is Collected

The Privacy Act requires that, when collecting personal information from individuals, agencies should provide those individuals with notice that includes the purpose for which the information was collected and the potential effect of not providing the information. Among other requirements, the act requires that the notification be located on the form the agency uses to collect information from the individual or on an accompanying form that the individual can keep, and that the notice cite the legal authority for the information request. According to OMB, this requirement is based on the assumption that individuals should be provided with sufficient information about the request to make a decision about whether to respond. The 1973 federal advisory committee report noted that the requirement was intended to discourage organizations from probing unnecessarily for details of people's lives under circumstances in which people may be reluctant to refuse to provide the requested data.

The agencies responsible for two of the five efforts we reviewed generally fulfilled the Privacy Act requirements regarding providing notice at the time of collection, one partially fulfilled these requirements, and two agencies claimed exemptions from these requirements. Table 6 details the steps agencies took to notify individuals when collecting personal information.

Table 6: Questions Related to Agency Actions to Notify Individuals at the Time Personal Information Was Collected

Question	Yes	Partial	No	Exempt
Were individuals notified of the legal authority that authorized the agency to collect the information?	E	A	B	CD
Were individuals notified of whether or not submitting information was mandatory or voluntary?	BE	A		CD
Were individuals notified of the principal purposes for which the information was to be used?	BE	A		CD
Were individuals notified of the routine uses for the information?	BE	A		CD
Were individuals notified of the effects, if any, of not supplying the information?	BE	A		CD

Legend:

A: RMA's data mining effort

B: State's Citibank Custom Reporting System

C: IRS's Reveal effort

D: FBI's Foreign Terrorist Tracking Task Force effort

E: SBA's Lender/Loan Monitoring System

Source: GAO analysis of agency information.

State and SBA generally provided the required notice when they collected personal information. Since May 2005, SBA has included a notice on applications for its loan programs that addressed the Privacy Act requirements. State provided notification using both a written notice on the purchase card application and a mandatory training program that all potential purchase cardholders must take before applying to the program. However, neither of the methods State used to notify employees identified the legal basis for the information request, as required by the Privacy Act. State officials told us that they were unaware that such a notice was required, but that they intend to notify employees of the legal basis in the future.

RMA also provided a notice on application forms, but these notices were not provided to everyone who supplied personal information. In the crop insurance program, participants apply for coverage from an insurance company that collects information from applicants and provides it to RMA. Because the information is collected on its behalf, RMA is responsible for ensuring that individuals receive the required notifications. However, RMA could not demonstrate that all individuals who provided it with data were properly notified. RMA provided documents showing that 16 of the 17 insurance providers included the disclosures required by the Privacy Act on the application forms they provided to borrowers. However, none of the lenders demonstrated that they provided adequate notice to insurance agents or adjusters, who also provided personal information used by RMA. According to RMA officials, they were unaware that this Privacy Act requirement applies to all the individuals about whom they collected information. When agencies do not fully notify individuals about the purpose and uses of the information they collect, the individuals have limited ability to make a reasonable decision about whether or not to supply the requested information.

FBI and IRS claimed allowable exemptions to the requirement to provide direct notice to individuals when they collect information under the Privacy Act because they use the collected information for law enforcement purposes.

Agencies' Actions to Ensure Security of Data Mining Efforts and Quality of Information They Used Were Inconsistent

The Privacy Act requires agencies to establish appropriate administrative, technical, and physical safeguards to ensure the security of records and to protect against any anticipated threats or hazards to their security that could result in substantial harm, embarrassment, inconvenience, or unfairness to any individual about whom information is maintained. While the act does not specify the types of procedures that agencies should take to ensure information security, FISMA and related OMB guidance define specific procedures for ensuring the security (which encompasses protections for availability, confidentiality, and integrity) of information. These procedures include performing risk assessments and developing security plans. Guidance from OMB and the National Institute of Standards and Technology (NIST) provide further detail on how agencies are to address security.

The Privacy Act also requires agencies to maintain all records used to make determinations about an individual with sufficient accuracy, relevance, timeliness, and completeness as is reasonably necessary to assure fairness. For the purposes of this report, we refer to these requirements as data quality requirements. According to OMB, this provision is intended to minimize the risk that an agency will make an adverse determination about an individual based on inaccurate, incomplete, or out-of-date records.

In the five efforts we reviewed, agency compliance with the security and data quality requirements was inconsistent. Table 7 summarizes the steps agencies took to ensure the security and accuracy of the information in the data mining efforts. Appendix VII provides additional detail on the specific actions that make up the key requirements and agencies' compliance with them.

Table 7: Questions Related to Agency Actions Safeguarding and Ensuring the Quality of Records Containing Personal Information

Question	Yes	Partial	No	Exempt
Has the agency performed a risk assessment to determine the information system vulnerabilities, identify threats, and develop countermeasures to those threats?	ACDE		B	
Has the agency developed a security plan for each system?	CD	AE	B	
Has the agency had the system(s) certified and accredited by management?	ADE		B	C[a]
Does the agency have a tested contingency plan for the system?	CE	AD	B	
Has the agency performed testing and evaluation of the data mining system(s)?	DE	AC[a]	B	
Did the agency take steps to ensure the accuracy, relevance, timeliness, and completeness of the data used to make determinations about individuals?	B	A		CDE[b]

Legend:

A: RMA's data mining effort

B: State's Citibank Custom Reporting System

C: IRS's Reveal effort

D: FBI's Foreign Terrorist Tracking Task Force effort

E: SBA's Lender/Loan Monitoring System

Source: GAO analysis of agency information.

[a]The IRS Reveal effort became operational in February 2005 and has interim authority to operate—not full certification and accreditation. IRS is currently testing the system.

[b]SBA's data mining effort is not used to make decisions about individuals.

Security. While the agencies responsible for the data mining efforts we reviewed followed a number of key security procedures, none had fully implemented all the procedures we evaluated. Although SBA, FBI, and RMA applied many of the key procedures required for the information systems used in their data mining efforts, their documentation did not include all the information called for in federal guidance. Specifically, SBA and RMA did not fully document its incident response capability, and neither FBI nor RMA demonstrated that their systems had tested contingency plans—a key requirement for adequate security planning. IRS produced several of the required security-related documents, but its documentation did not demonstrate that all of the underlying requirements had been met. IRS's system became operational in February 2005 and is currently undergoing testing.

Neither of the two agencies responsible for State's data mining effort took the steps required to ensure that the information systems used in the effort had adequate security. As the contracting agency for the governmentwide purchase card program, GSA is responsible for ensuring that information and information systems used in the program—including those provided by contractors—follow FISMA guidance. However, according to agency officials, GSA has not evaluated vendors' systems for compliance with the specific provisions of FISMA; instead, GSA currently relies on the banks to provide security and on the Office of the Comptroller of the Currency[15] for oversight of the banks.

Because State uses an information system operated by Citibank, through its task order under the purchase card program contract, FISMA requires that State ensure that Citibank's system complies with FISMA provisions. While State performed a general review of Citibank's security processes before starting to use its systems, State did not specifically evaluate Citibank's compliance with federal security requirements. Agencies that do not take adequate steps to ensure information security risk having information improperly exposed, altered, or destroyed. For example, another bank participating in a related program lost backup tapes containing personal information on government employees.[16] GSA program officials noted that they were satisfied that the situation was an accident and not a reflection of a significant security failing on the bank's part.

Data quality. State took steps to ensure that the information used in its data mining efforts is accurate, relevant, timely, and complete. State used a monthly review process whereby cardholders review the account statements provided by Citibank for accuracy. The same information is also

---

[15]The Office of the Comptroller of the Currency, a component of the Department of the Treasury, is responsible for oversight of nationally chartered banks and state and federally chartered savings associations. The office is responsible for auditing federally insured institutions under its jurisdiction annually. The audit, in part, evaluates the institution's safety and soundness; determines compliance with applicable laws, rules, and regulations; and ensures that it maintains capital commensurate with its risk.

[16]The recent incident involved Bank of America's loss of data regarding the government travel card program.

reviewed by the cardholders' supervisors. In addition, area program coordinators must review the purchase card programs in their area annually.

RMA took steps that partially ensure the quality of the data in its data mining effort; for example, it has an editing and data validation process in place. However, while this process addresses the accuracy of the system's data, it does not address the relevance, timeliness or completeness of the personal information in the data mining system because program officials were unaware of the requirement to do so. Those agencies that do not take adequate steps to ensure the quality of the information they use and collect risk making unwarranted decisions based on inaccurate information.

The provision regarding data quality did not apply to three efforts. SBA does not use the information in its data mining effort to make determinations about individuals; rather, it uses it to manage groups of loans. FBI and IRS claimed an allowable exemption because their records are used for criminal law enforcement. According to the rule justifying FBI's exemption, it is impossible to make such determinations in part because information that may initially appear to be untimely or irrelevant can acquire new significance as an investigation proceeds.

Five Agencies Lacked Comprehensive Privacy Impact Assessments for Their Data Mining Efforts

The E-Government Act of 2002 requires that federal government agencies conduct privacy impact assessments before developing or procuring information technology or initiating any new electronic data collections containing personal information on 10 or more individuals. According to OMB, such assessments help agencies to

- determine whether the agency's information handling practices conform to the established legal, regulatory, and policy requirements regarding privacy;

- evaluate risks arising from electronic collection and maintenance of information about individuals; and

- evaluate protections or alternative processes needed to mitigate the risks identified.

Thus, a timely and comprehensive privacy impact assessment can be used by agencies as a tool to ensure not only strict compliance with the various laws related to privacy, but also as a means to consider broader privacy principles, such as the fair information practices that formed the basis for those laws.

The E-Government Act lays out a series of requirements for assessments, such as (1) they must describe and analyze how the information is secured, (2) they must describe and analyze the intended uses of information, (3) the agency's chief information officer (or designee) must review the assessment, and (4) the assessment must be publicly available unless making it so would raise security concerns or reveal sensitive or classified information. OMB guidance does not require privacy impact assessments for systems used for internal government operations or for national security systems; however, individual agencies may have more stringent privacy impact assessment requirements.

While four of the five agencies were required to conduct assessments by statute or by agency rule, three (RMA, SBA, and IRS) did so. However, none of these assessments adequately addressed all the statutory requirements. Table 8 summarizes agency actions to assess the privacy impacts of their data mining efforts.

Table 8: Questions Related to Agency Actions to Conduct Privacy Impact Assessments

Question	Yes	Partial	No	Exempt
Was a privacy impact assessment prepared?	ACE		D	B[b]
Did the privacy impact assessment describe and analyze what information was to be collected?		ACE	D	B[b]
Did the privacy impact assessment describe and analyze why the information was to be collected?		AC	DE	B[b]
Did the privacy impact assessment describe and analyze the intended use of the information?		AC	DE	B[b]
Did the privacy impact assessment describe and analyze with whom the collected information was to be shared?		ACE	D	B[b]
Did the privacy impact assessment describe and analyze the notice or opportunity for consent for individuals impacted by the system?			ADE	C[a]B[b]
Did the privacy impact assessment describe and analyze how the information was to be secured?		ACE	D	B[b]
Did the privacy impact assessment describe and analyze whether a Privacy Act system of records is being created?		ACE	D	B[b]

(Continued From Previous Page)

Question	Yes	Partial	No	Exempt
Did the privacy impact assessment identify the choices the agency made as a result of performing the assessment?		C	ADE	B[b]
Was the privacy impact assessment reviewed by the agency's chief information officer or his/her equivalent?	C		ADE	B[b]
Was the privacy impact assessment made publicly available?	E	C	AD	B[b]

Legend:

A: RMA's data mining effort

B: State's Citibank Custom Reporting System

C: IRS's Reveal effort

D: FBI's Foreign Terrorist Tracking Task Force effort

E: SBA's Lender/Loan Monitoring System

Source: GAO analysis of agency information.

[a]The IRS Reveal system is exempt from giving notice at the time of collection based on a law enforcement exemption to the Privacy Act.

[b]OMB guidance does not require privacy impact assessments for internal government systems.

Three agencies conducted assessments that partially addressed the requirements. For example, while RMA's plan addressed the information to be collected and how it was to be used, it did not receive the required review by the agency chief information officer or designee. In addition, RMA's assessment was not made publicly available, even though the document did not include any sensitive information.[17] IRS's notice stated that it would use the information for queries, but did not analyze the purpose for collecting the information or its intended uses, as required. For instance, IRS's privacy impact assessment states that the system "is used to identify potential criminal investigations of individuals or groups" in "support of the overall IRS mission." While this describes the purpose for collecting the information and its intended uses, it does not analyze how the agency reached these decisions. RMA and IRS did not fully address these steps because they used a prior version of guidance that did not address all the current requirements when conducting their assessments. SBA conducted an assessment of a previous loan monitoring effort that

---

[17]Under OMB guidance, an agency may decide not to make the PIA document or summary publicly available to the extent that publication would raise security concerns or reveal classified (i.e., national security) or sensitive information (e.g., potentially damaging to a national interest, law enforcement effort, or competitive business interest) contained in an assessment.

addressed several aspects of their current data mining effort. This assessment included general descriptions of what information was to be collected, why the information was to be collected, the intended use of the information, and how the information was to be secured. However, the assessment did not analyze these decisions, as required by OMB's guidance. According to SBA officials, the privacy assessment was not more specific because at the time it was completed, the possible uses of the system and the format it would take were not certain. SBA officials added that a more specific privacy assessment of the data mining effort has been drafted and is expected to be published later in the current fiscal year.

FBI has not conducted a privacy impact assessment for its data mining effort. FBI is not required by statute to conduct assessments on these systems because they are classified as national security systems. However, under FBI regulations, assessments are required for these systems. According to agency officials, FBI is in the process of preparing privacy assessments for the two systems that make up its data mining effort, but these assessments were delayed due to competing priorities for its operational support team. The officials said that the agency does not have a target date for completing the assessments.

The lack of comprehensive assessments is a missed opportunity for agencies to ensure that the data mining efforts we reviewed are subject to the most appropriate privacy protections. Because the assessments did not address all the required subjects, including those related to several Privacy Act provisions, agencies were sometimes unaware that they were not following all the requirements of the act. Further, without analyses regarding their approaches to privacy protection, agencies have little assurance that their approaches reflect the appropriate balance between individual privacy rights and the operational needs of the government.

GSA, the contracting agency for the governmentwide purchase card program, did not conduct a privacy assessment because OMB guidance does not require them for internal government programs. However, OMB guidance encourages agencies to conduct privacy impact assessments on systems that collect information in identifiable form about government personnel. Further, according to agency officials, GSA is developing guidance requiring assessments for all new agency systems which will apply to the purchase card program.

Conclusions

The five data mining efforts illustrate ways in which federal agencies collect and use personal information for purposes such as program oversight and law enforcement. The agencies responsible for these data mining efforts took many of the key steps required to protect the privacy and security of the personal information they used. However, none of the agencies followed all the key privacy and security provisions we reviewed. Those that did not apply key privacy protections limited the ability of the public—including those individuals whose information was used—to participate in the management of that personal information. Those agencies that did not apply the appropriate security protections increased the risk that personal information could be improperly exposed or altered. Until agencies fully comply with the Privacy Act, they lack assurance that individual privacy rights are appropriately protected.

Further, none of the agencies we reviewed conducted a complete privacy impact assessment. Had their assessments fully addressed the required Privacy Act provisions, the agencies would have had an opportunity to identify and remedy areas of noncompliance. In addition, none of the privacy impact assessments adequately addressed the choices that agencies made regarding privacy in their data mining efforts. As a result, the basis for their choices regarding tradeoffs between privacy protections and operational needs is unclear. Better analyses of such choices could help agencies strike the appropriate balance between operational needs and individuals' rights to privacy.

Recommendations

To ensure that the data mining efforts reviewed include adequate privacy protections, we are making 19 recommendations to the agencies responsible for them. Specifically, we recommend that the Secretary of Agriculture direct the Administrator of the Risk Management Agency (RMA) to

- provide the required Privacy Act notices to individuals, including producers, insurance agents, and adjusters, when personal information is collected from them;

- apply the appropriate information security measures defined in OMB and NIST guidance to the systems used in the RMA data mining effort, specifically, the development of a complete system security plan, a tested contingency plan, and regular testing and evaluation of the systems used in the effort;

- develop and implement procedures that ensure the accuracy, relevance, timeliness, and completeness of personal information used in the RMA data mining effort to make determinations about individuals;

- revise the privacy impact assessment for the RMA data mining effort to comply with OMB guidance, including analyses of the intended use of the information it collects, with whom the information will be shared, how the information is to be secured, opportunities for impacted individuals to comment, and the choices made by the agency as a result of the assessment;

- have the completed privacy impact assessment approved by the chief information officer or equivalent official; and

- make the completed privacy impact assessment available to the public, as appropriate.

We recommend that the Secretary of the Treasury direct the Commissioner of the Internal Revenue Service to

- apply the appropriate information security measures defined in OMB and NIST guidance to the systems used in the Reveal data mining effort, specifically, the performance of regular system testing and evaluation against NIST guidance;

- revise the privacy impact assessment for the Internal Revenue Service's Reveal system to comply with OMB guidance, including analyses of the information to be collected, the purposes of the collection, the intended use of the information, how the information is to be secured, and opportunities for impacted individuals to comment; and

- make the completed privacy impact assessment available to the public, as appropriate.

We recommend that the Attorney General direct the Director of the Federal Bureau of Investigation to

- apply the appropriate information security measures defined in OMB and NIST guidance to the systems used in the Foreign Terrorist Tracking Task Force data mining effort, including the development of tested contingency plans;

- establish a date for the completion of a privacy impact assessment for its data mining effort that complies with OMB guidance, including analyses of the information to be collected, the purposes of the collection, the intended use of the information, with whom information will be shared, how the information is to be secured, opportunities for impacted individuals to comment, and the choices made by the agency as a result of the assessment;

- have the completed privacy impact assessment approved by the chief information officer or equivalent official; and

- make the completed privacy impact assessment available to the public, as appropriate.

We recommend that the Secretary of State direct the Under Secretary for Management to notify purchase card participants of the legal basis under which the department collects their personal information, as required.

We recommend that the Administrator of the Small Business Administration

- amend the system of records notice regarding its data mining effort to clearly identify the individual responsible for the effort, the process by which individuals can request notification that the system includes records about them, and the procedures individuals should use to review records pertaining to them;

- complete a privacy impact assessment for the data mining effort that complies with OMB guidance, including analyses of the information to be collected, the purposes of the collection, the intended use of the information, how the information is to be secured, opportunities for impacted individuals to comment, and the choices made by the agency as a result of the assessment; and

- make the completed privacy impact assessment available to the public, as appropriate.

We recommend that the Administrator of the General Services Administration

- publish a system of records notice for the purchase card program that specifies the name of the system, the categories of individuals and records in the system, the categories of information sources used by the system, the routine uses of the system, how the agency stores and maintains the system, the individual responsible for the effort, the process by which individuals can request notification that the system includes records about them, and the procedures individuals should use to review records pertaining to them and

- ensure that the appropriate information security measures defined in OMB and NIST guidance are applied to the systems used in the Citibank Custom Reporting System data mining effort, including the development of a risk assessment, a system security plan, a tested contingency plan, the performance of regular testing and evaluation, and the completion of certification and accreditation by agency management.

Agency Comments and Our Evaluation

We provided Agriculture, Treasury, Justice, State, SBA, and GSA with a draft of this report for their review and comment. We received written comments on the report and its recommendations from SBA, Agriculture, State, and Treasury, and comments via e-mail from GSA's Assistant Commissioner for Acquisition. These agencies generally agreed with the majority of our recommendations, but disagreed with others. Justice's Senior Audit Liaison stated that the department had no comments. Agriculture, IRS, State, and SBA also provided technical comments, which we addressed as appropriate.

The Administrator, RMA, stated that RMA agreed with the majority of our recommendations and that the agency had taken steps to implement many of them. In response to our recommendation that RMA strengthen security measures, the Administrator stated that RMA has a security plan for its data mining system and performs regular testing and evaluation. While our draft indicated that RMA had implemented some of the necessary security measures, we noted that it did not follow all related guidance. Specifically, the system security plan did not describe its incident response capability, and RMA did not document that it had conducted annual testing or that its tests included penetration or vulnerability testing. We clarified this recommendation to focus on the incomplete and undocumented security measures we identified. In response to our recommendation that RMA develop and implement procedures that ensure the quality of personal information used in its data mining system, USDA commented that they already have an editing and validation process in place. We clarified the discussion of this point in our report. However, while this process addresses the accuracy of the system's data, it does not address the relevance, timeliness or completeness of the personal information in the data mining system. USDA's comments are contained in appendix VIII.

Treasury's Chief Information Officer generally agreed with our recommendations regarding a privacy impact assessment, and said that IRS will conduct a new privacy impact assessment that complies with current OMB guidance after Reveal becomes operational. While conducting a new privacy impact assessment is an appropriate step, we note that the E-Government Act and OMB guidance require that assessments be conducted before systems become operational. In responding to our recommendation to ensure that appropriate security measures are applied to IRS's Reveal data mining effort, Treasury stated that Reveal is in compliance with OMB, NIST, and Treasury security guidance and is operating under an interim authorization to operate while it undergoes certification and accreditation. Our report acknowledges that IRS had applied several security measures, but also notes that required regular testing and evaluation was not yet in place. We clarified this recommendation to focus on these requirements. Treasury's comments are contained in appendix IX.

State's Assistant Secretary and Chief Financial Officer generally agreed with our recommendation that it notify purchase card participants of the legal basis under which the Department collects their personal information; State responded that it will take the necessary steps to address this recommendation. In addition, regarding a recommendation we made to GSA concerning the Citibank Custom Reporting System, State raised the issue of whether a privacy impact assessment is required for systems that collect information on federal employees, as is the case with this system. As discussed below in our response to GSA, we agree that OMB guidance exempts internal government systems from the requirement to conduct privacy impact assessments and have clarified our report to reflect this. State's comments are contained in appendix X.

SBA's Associate Deputy Administrator for Office of Capital Access generally agreed with our recommendations and provided information on its planned actions. SBA's comments are contained in appendix XI.

GSA's Assistant Commissioner for Acquisition generally disagreed with our recommendations. He stated that GSA has not published a system of records notice for the purchase card program because this program does not capture personal information. However, as described in the report, the system retrieves information about individuals by personal identifiers, and thus meets the Privacy Act's definition of a system of records. In commenting on our recommendation that GSA ensure that appropriate security measures defined in OMB and NIST guidance are applied to the data mining effort, GSA explained that they have reviewed the security standards of the five financial institutions on the GSA SmartPay master contract, and have concluded that the commercial standards and procedures provided by these institutions offer the Citibank Custom Reporting System sufficient security protection. However, GSA is required to ensure that information and information systems used in the program—including those provided by contractors—meet the requirements of FISMA, including the implementing guidance from OMB and NIST. Further, recent OMB guidance requires agencies to ensure implementation of security measures identical to those required under FISMA. GSA also provided a security risk assessment of the security in the SmartPay Master Contract. However, the assessment does not address any of the elements of the NIST guidance for implementing risk assessments, such as identifying the system's vulnerabilities and threats. Finally, in response to our three recommendations regarding the requirement to conduct a privacy impact assessment, the Assistant Commissioner stated that GSA is not required to conduct a privacy impact assessment because it is contracting for a financial system, not an IT system. Because it is an internal government system, we agree that GSA is not required by OMB guidance to conduct a privacy impact assessment on the Citibank system and have clarified our report to reflect this.

As agreed with your office, unless you publicly release the contents of this report earlier, we plan no further distribution until 30 days from the report date. We will send copies of this report to the Chairmen and Ranking Minority Members of other Senate and House committees and subcommittees that have jurisdiction and oversight responsibility for SBA, Agriculture, State, Treasury, GSA, and Justice. Copies will be made available to others on request. In addition, this report will be available at no charge on the GAO Web site at http://www.gao.gov.

If you have any questions concerning this report, please contact me at (202) 512-6240 or by e-mail at koontzl@gao.gov. Contact points for our Offices of Congressional Relations and Public Affairs may be found on the last page of this report. GAO staff who made major contributions to this report are listed in appendix XII.

Sincerely yours,

Linda D. Koontz
Director, Information Management Issues

Scope and Methodology

To address our objectives, we used a case study methodology. We selected the data mining efforts to be included in our evaluations from the 122 federal data mining systems reported to us in 2004.[1] In that report, we identified the six most common purposes for the data mining activities reported to us. For the purposes of this review, we excluded systems used for two purposes: we did not select any systems used for analyzing scientific and research information because few of those systems used personal information, and we excluded systems used for managing human resources because such records fall under different privacy rules and regulations.

The remaining four most common purposes were

- improving service or performance;

- detecting fraud, waste, and abuse;

- detecting criminal activities or patterns; and

- analyzing intelligence and detecting terrorist activities.

From the systems that were used for these purposes, we selected all those that met each of the following criteria:

- used personal identifiers,

- were operational, and

- used data from another agency or private sector data.

These criteria were chosen to ensure that the efforts we selected illustrated agency practices regarding personal information. In addition, we selected no more than one system from each department or agency.

We analyzed the information provided in 2004 and determined that 11 data mining efforts met all of our initial selection criteria. We contacted the agencies responsible for the systems to confirm the accuracy of the information previously provided. As a result of the updated information, we

---

[1]See GAO, *Data Mining: Federal Efforts Cover a Wide Range of Uses*, GAO-04-548 (Washington, D.C.: May 4, 2004).

eliminated from consideration several systems that no longer met all of the selection criteria, resulting in the final selection of five data mining systems for our case study review.

To describe the characteristics of the selected federal data mining efforts, we analyzed system documentation, public notices, and other relevant documents and interviewed officials at the responsible department or agency, and, when applicable, the supporting contractor. Agency officials were provided with several opportunities to review our descriptions of the selected systems and the graphical depictions included in appendixes II through VI.

To determine whether agencies provided adequate privacy protection for the personal information used in the selected data mining efforts, we analyzed federal privacy and security laws, regulations, and other guidance to identify key steps and procedures for protecting the privacy of individual information. We then developed a data collection instrument consisting of a series of questions about agency actions that followed the key steps and procedures, as well as questions on the detailed characteristics of the data mining systems, and provided the instrument to the responsible agencies. We reviewed the agencies' responses and any supporting documentation they provided, and assigned an answer of yes (compliant with all of the guidance related to that question), no (not compliant with any of the guidance related to that question), or partial (compliant with some, but not all of the guidance) to each question. We also reviewed rules claiming exemptions. We discussed the results with agency officials and made adjustments as appropriate.

Because we studied only five data mining efforts and because of the method of selection, we cannot conclude that our results represent any larger group of data mining efforts. Although they were not representative of all federal data mining efforts, we believe that the five efforts we reviewed illustrate some of the ways in which agencies satisfy federal privacy provisions and the circumstances under which agencies can claim exemptions to these provisions.

We conducted our work from May 2004 to June 2005 at the Washington, D.C., area offices of the Departments of State and Agriculture, Internal Revenue Service, Federal Bureau of Investigation, Small Business Administration, and General Services Administration, at an agency facility in Philadelphia, Pennsylvania, and at the Stephenville, Texas, location of an agency contractor. Our work was conducted in accordance with generally accepted government auditing standards.

Risk Management Agency's Data Mining Effort

The Risk Management Agency[1] (RMA) uses a data mining system designed by Tarleton State University's Center for Agribusiness Excellence (CAE) to assist it in detecting fraud, waste, and abuse in the federal crop insurance program. The data mining system is used to identify producers, insurance agents, and loss adjusters who may be abusing the program. Its inputs include insurance records on policy holders, agents, and loss adjusters, as well as data on soil, weather, and land. It produces several types of outputs, including lists of names of individuals whose behavior is anomalous.

Purpose and Uses

The purpose of the RMA data mining system is to detect fraud, waste, and abuse in the federal crop insurance program by investigating potential leads and confirming suspicious activity in high-profile cases.[2] It also uses the system to improve program policies, guidance, and data quality. According to RMA officials, the system significantly augmented agency program integrity initiatives and accounted for over $340 million in cost avoidance savings since its inception.

According to RMA officials, CAE analysts identify potential abusers of the federal crop insurance program primarily by developing scenarios of abuse of the program by producers, insurance agents, and loss adjusters. Analysts query the data warehouse by using data mining and pattern recognition techniques to identify information, patterns, anomalies, or relationships indicative of fraud, waste, and abuse. CAE analysts then generate reports for RMA regional compliance offices, which use the reports to determine which producers should be inspected for potential abuse.

RMA uses reports produced by the data mining system for policy development in the *Crop Insurance Handbook* and improvement of the federal crop insurance program. RMA's officials often request data mining reports (1) to help evaluate pilot programs before making policy changes, (2) to determine the best way to change program procedures once the policies are implemented, and (3) to determine ways to enhance the data through quality control reviews.

---

[1]The Risk Management Agency is a component of the U.S. Department of Agriculture.

[2]The federal crop insurance program is designed to protect farmers from financial losses caused by events such as droughts, floods, hurricanes, and other natural disasters as well as losses resulting from a drop in crop prices. RMA administers and oversees the federal crop insurance program.

How It Works

RMA's data mining effort uses a data warehouse containing crop insurance data and information from weather, soil, and land survey sources to develop and conduct pattern-based searches for identifying information, patterns, anomalies, or relationships indicative of fraud, waste, and abuse. Pattern-based searches are based on scenarios of fraudulent schemes for obtaining crop insurance indemnities (the dollar amount paid in the event of an insured loss) that are developed by analysts and agricultural experts. The data mining system helps analysts uncover these patterns through an iterative process. Each scenario is tested and refined by querying data in the warehouse. The results are then provided to a CAE product review team that approves or rejects the scenario. Once a scenario is approved, analysts can use it to search the data warehouse for individuals who match the scenario patterns. Analysts use multiple scenarios to query the data warehouse in order to identify program participants who are potentially involved in fraudulent activities, resulting in a "spot check list."

Table 9 lists (1) the names and attributes of the scenarios developed by RMA and CAE and (2) the agency-reported summary of potentially fraudulent claims reported by producers whose behavior was identified as anomalous on the 2002 spot check list. According to RMA officials, the eight scenarios listed in table 9 have been the most successful in generating program savings.

Table 9: Scenarios Used to Identify Potential Abusers

Dollars in millions

Scenario name	Scenario characteristics	Summary of the 2002 spot check list: potentially fraudulent claims
Triplets	Agents, adjusters, and producers linked by anomalous behavior that is suggestive of collusion.	$4.3
Rare big losses	Producers who make claims much too often compared to other producers of the same crop in the same area.	32.8
Under-reported harvest production	Producers who hide part of their production by reporting it under someone else's name or by growing a crop on land hidden from inspectors. They are compared only to other producers who experienced the same weather conditions.	23.5
Frequent filers	Anomalous producers reporting consecutive multiyear losses. They make claims for seven consecutive years and their indemnities each year are at least as high as their insurance premiums.	21.7
Yield switching	Producers whose yield difference (the difference between their rate yield and actual reported yield) is—over a period of years—significantly above or significantly below other producers in the same area for the same crop.	15.5
All or nothing	Insurance agents whose losses on their policyholders' crop insurance policies are disproportionately higher than those of agents in the same area.	12.2
Prevented planting	Producers who grow crops outside the planting schedule required by the *Federal Crop Insurance Handbook*[a] and file a claim for not being able to produce the crop.	7.0
Excessive yield	Producers with crop units that have excessive reported yields when compared to those of agents in the same area.	36.2

Source: RMA.

[a]The *Federal Crop Insurance Handbook* contains underwriting standards for administering crop insurance policies under RMA's oversight.

RMA's six regional compliance offices use the data mining query results, including the spot check list, to determine which producers should be inspected for potential abuse. Once the regional compliance offices review the list, they forward it to employees of USDA's Farm Service Agency who send notification letters to the producers on the list, alerting them to pending inspections. According to RMA officials, the notice of a pending inspection is often enough to discourage the producers from filing fraudulent claims. Figure 2 depicts this process.

Figure 2: An Overview of the RMA System

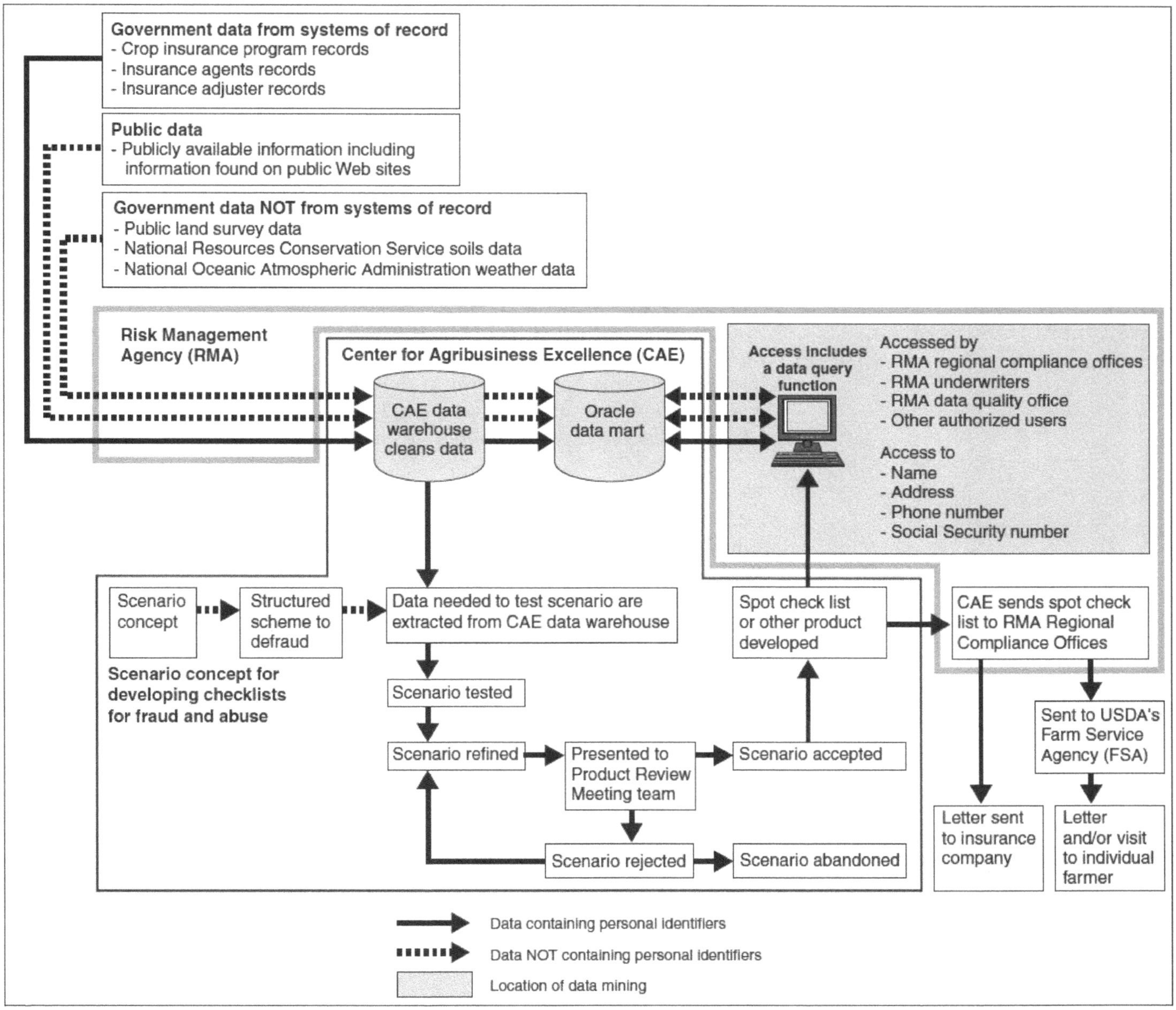

Source: GAO analysis of agency data.

Inputs	The RMA data mining effort uses government data covered by systems of records notices, including crop insurance data. Data in the RMA system not from systems of records include public land, weather, and soils data. In addition to government data, RMA uses other publicly available information on an as-needed basis.
Government Data from Systems of Records	*Crop Insurance Information.* Insurance companies participating in the program provide crop insurance information to RMA on program participants, including producers, insurance agents, and loss adjusters. The crop insurance data contains personal identifiers that can be linked to program participants, including names, addresses, phone numbers, and Social Security numbers.
Government Data Not from Systems of Records	*Land Survey Data.* The system uses digital maps from the Public Land Survey System—regulated by the Bureau of Land Management[3]—that depict public survey information, such as township locations referred to in legal land descriptions. Analysts use this information to determine whether there is a discrepancy between a producer's claim and land records.
	Weather Data. RMA uses information from public weather records from the National Oceanic and Atmospheric Administration to assist in validating specific causes of loss for further investigation.
	Soils Data. RMA plans to uses soils data from USDA's Natural Resources Conservation Service when determining whether soil on a producer's land is acceptable for growing an insured crop.
Public Data	The agency also uses other publicly available information including information found on public Web sites.
Outputs	RMA's data mining system produces reports for program investigators on producers whose behavior patterns are anomalous. The system also produces reports for program managers that include programmatic information—such as how a procedural change in the federal crop insurance program's policy manual would affect the overall effectiveness of

---

[3]The Bureau of Land Management is a Department of the Interior agency that manages 264 million surface acres of public lands located primarily in 12 western states, including Alaska.

the program—and other information on data quality and program performance.

The Citibank Custom Reporting System Used by the Department of State

The U.S. Department of State (State) contracts with Citibank through the General Services Administration's GSA SmartPay[1] contract to provide State employees with purchase cards.[2] Under the contract, Citibank provides State and other contracting agencies access to the Citibank Custom Reporting System (CCRS)—a proprietary tool designed by Citibank. State uses this system to analyze transaction data and help prevent fraud, waste, and abuse in its purchase card program. The system's inputs include account information from State employees and commercial data from transactions made by State employees. System outputs include summaries of card account holder information and purchases.

Purpose and Uses

The purpose of State's data mining effort is to prevent fraud, waste, and abuse in the purchase card program by using CCRS to ensure that credit and purchase limits are in place and to conduct spot checks of individual purchase card expenditures.[3] Officials also use the system to improve program performance through the results of simple subject- and pattern-based queries.[4]

According to State officials, the department uses reports containing information on agency purchase card accounts and suspended or cancelled accounts. State officials also regularly review a CCRS report that summarizes single transaction and monthly spending limits for all cardholders to ensure that they are accurate. According to State officials, one of the most important tasks accomplished through system reports is ensuring that the ratio of cardholders to approving officials—a cardholder's

---

[1] In 1998, GSA awarded contracts to five major banks through the GSA SmartPay program to provide federal agencies with purchase cards as well as travel cards and cards for fleet-related expenses. The participating banks are Bank of America, Bank One (now J.P. Morgan Chase), Citibank, Mellon Bank, and U.S. Bank. Individual agencies select one of the participating banks and issue a task order to the bank based on the terms of the master contract with GSA.

[2] Purchase cards are bank charge cards used primarily for purchases totaling less than $2,500.

[3] State is the lead U.S. foreign affairs agency and operates more than 250 posts around the world. State employees use purchase cards to make work-related purchases in support of State's mission.

[4] Users can use subject-based queries to receive reports on an individual account's expenditures and can use pattern-based queries to determine, among other things, which vendors employees make purchases from.

immediate supervisor—is low enough for expenditures to be effectively reviewed.

According to State officials, the department also uses reports to assist with overall purchase card program management functions. These reports provide the ability to track overall purchase card expenditures by a number of data elements, including spending by region or embassy, or by vendors used by State employees. State also uses CCRS to collect and compile statistical information about the program for quarterly reports submitted to the Office of Management and Budget. These reports include information on the number of current accounts, dollars spent, rebate amounts earned, and single purchase and monthly expenditure limits for cardholders.

How It Works

The CCRS electronic reporting tool is a Citibank proprietary system. The system interfaces with Citibank's Global Data Repository, which stores account and transaction data for an 18-month period. A portion of the data resulting from the transaction process is replicated in the primary system database for use in analysis and report preparation. Figure 3 illustrates the transaction process. Reports can be printed or downloaded from the system; the presentation of the data can be edited within the system, or the data can be downloaded to be analyzed in an outside program.

When using the system, State users can access reports developed in the system, including reports of purchase card accounts, suspended or cancelled accounts, and summary reports on the vendors State employees purchase from. Reports not already established in the system can be created by Citibank at the request of agency officials. Figure 3 illustrates this process.

Figure 3: An Overview of the Citibank Custom Reporting System

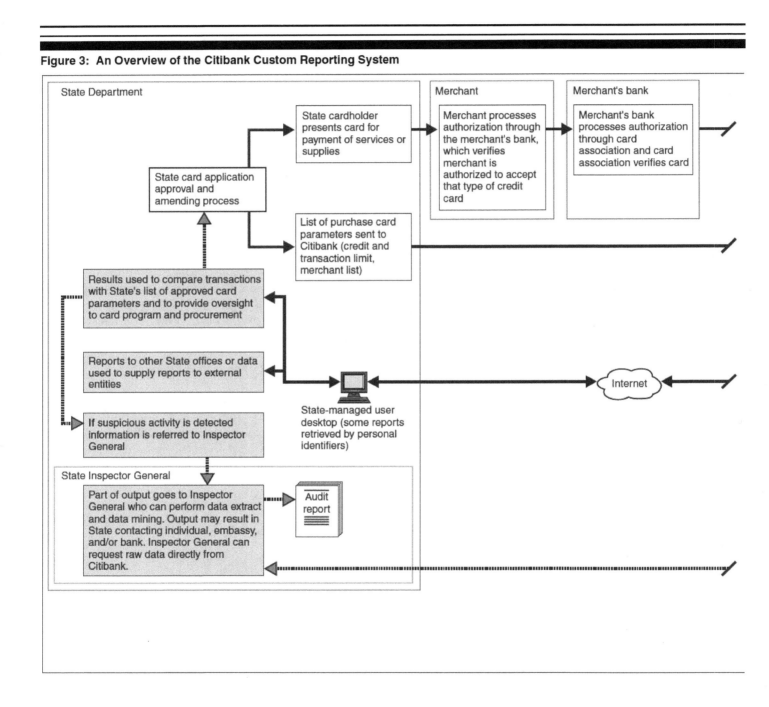

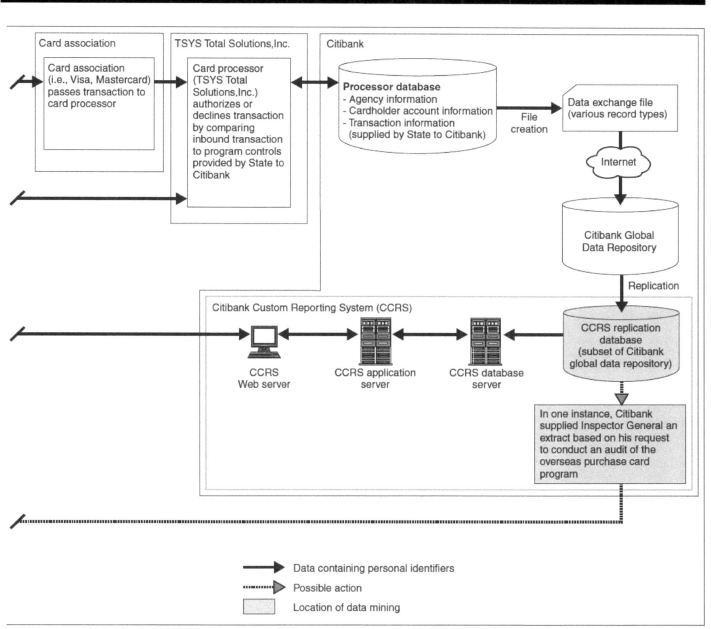

Source: GAO analysis of agency data.

Inputs	CCRS includes transaction and account data. Account data are collected from agency employees, with an account number issued by Citibank; transaction data consist of records of purchase card transactions conducted by State employees.
Government Data Not from Systems of Records	*Account Data.* State collects personal information, including name, last four digits of the Social Security number, and the cardholder's office phone number and mailing and e-mail addresses as part of the purchase card application process. According to agency officials, State retrieves records by cardholder name. State supplies that information to Citibank. State also supplies required account parameters—such as single transaction and monthly spending limits—and assigns a unique identifying number. Other account information is assigned by Citibank.[5]
Commercial Data	*Transaction Data.* The amount and level of detail available in the transaction data varies depending on the technical capabilities of the vendor from whom products are purchased. For example, vendors with the most basic capabilities transfer standard commercial transaction data, including the total purchase amount, date of purchase, vendor's name and location, date the charge or credit was processed, and a reference number for each charge or credit. Vendors with more advanced technology can provide additional information including, among other things, unit cost and quantity, vendor's category code, and sales tax amount.
Outputs	CCRS provides reports on purchase card transactions and account information, including a list of all purchase card accounts, a report on suspended or cancelled accounts, and reports summarizing expenditures by region or by vendor. Many reports in the CCRS system are available in a summary form that does not contain personal identifiers and in a detailed form containing personal identifiers, including account number and name.

According to State officials, CCRS reports are used within State's purchase card office to ensure adequacy and accuracy of compensating controls |

---

[5]Account data from the purchase card program are not covered by a system of records notice. See p. 17 for more information.

such as credit limits. Reports are also used to track expenditures and are supplied to other State offices, such as State's Inspector General, for use in analyzing purchases.

Internal Revenue Service's Reveal System

The Internal Revenue Service[1] (IRS) uses the Reveal system to detect patterns of criminal activity, analyze intelligence, and detect terrorist activities. According to agency officials, IRS uses the system to identify financial crime, including individual and corporate tax fraud, and terrorist activity. Inputs for Reveal include Bank Secrecy Act data, tax information, and counterterrorism information. Its outputs include reports containing names, Social Security numbers, addresses, and other personal information of individuals suspected of financial crime or terrorist activity.

Purpose and Uses

The purpose of the Reveal data mining system is to detect criminal activities and patterns in support of IRS's work in investigating potential criminal violations of the Internal Revenue Code and related financial crimes. This work is conducted by IRS's Criminal Investigation unit. According to agency officials, Reveal is used to analyze available databases to support ongoing investigations relating to financial crime, including individual and corporate tax fraud, and terrorist activity.

The system provides the capability to query data from multiple sources in an effort to identify links in the data. System users develop reports that include query results and graphical depictions of the data. The reports are then provided to field offices, which conduct investigations based on the reports' results.

The system allows users to establish a profile of the actions and persons associated with the search subject by allowing the user to trace numerous financial transactions between individuals and institutions.

How It Works

Reveal uses commercial software to query multiple databases. The system provides Criminal Investigation users with a visual depiction of the results, and allows them to search on names, Social Security numbers, and other information to help narrow their search. Reveal consists of (1) a data retrieval and manipulation tool that performs queries and (2) a software tool that provides a visual depiction of the query results. The retrieval and manipulation tool queries and gathers information on large sets of data that reside locally on a relational database on the system's database server. This tool allows users to sort, group, and export data from multiple information repositories simultaneously, including combinations of databases. It also

---

[1]The Internal Revenue Service is a bureau of the Department of the Treasury.

can perform two kinds of queries: reactive and proactive. To perform a reactive query, the user must provide a known value of an individual or entities. To perform a proactive query, the user narrows the search criteria to identify groups of individuals and patterns of suspicious activity.

When users narrow their search criteria using the query tool, they can use the visualization component to refine and assess the results of the queries. The software visualization tool shows relationships between data in the queries, and facilitates the discovery of relationships among entities, patterns, and trends in the data. It also organizes and presents the information in a variety of graphical formats. Figure 4 depicts this process.

Inputs

Reveal currently uses government system of records data as its only type of input. These inputs include (1) Bank Secrecy Act data, (2) tax data, and (3) counterterrorism data. These three types of data all contain personal information, such as address, Social Security number, and date of birth. Data sets are copied and stored locally.

Figure 4: An Overview of the Reveal Data Mining System

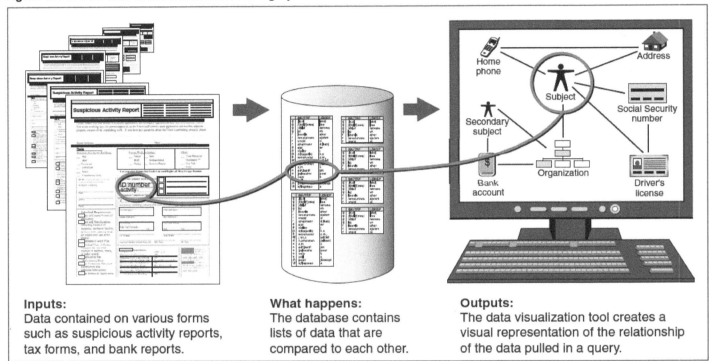

Inputs:
Data contained on various forms such as suspicious activity reports, tax forms, and bank reports.

What happens:
The database contains lists of data that are compared to each other.

Outputs:
The data visualization tool creates a visual representation of the relationship of the data pulled in a query.

Source: GAO analysis of agency data, Booz Allen Hamilton.

Government Data from Systems of Records

Bank Secrecy Act Data. Bank Secrecy Act (BSA)[2] data are accessed remotely from databases owned by the Financial Crimes Enforcement Network (FinCEN).[3] It consists of Suspicious Activity Reports submitted for a transaction related to a possible violation of a law or regulation.[4] BSA data also include Currency Transaction Reports which are filed by casinos for cash transactions in excess of $10,000 and by financial institutions for payments or transfers in excess of $10,000.

---

[2]The Bank Secrecy Act requires banks and other financial institutions to keep records and file reports that are useful in criminal, tax, and regulatory investigations or proceedings.

[3]FinCEN's mission is to safeguard the financial system from financial crime, and abuses including terrorist financing, money laundering, and other illicit activity.

[4]Suspicious Activity Reports are filed by (1) financial institutions, (2) money service businesses, (3) security and futures industries, and (4) casinos and card clubs.

Tax Data. Tax data used by Reveal include information from IRS's Schedule K-1, corporate and individual tax information, and applications for employer and tax identification numbers. It is used to report a beneficiary's share of income, deductions, and credits from a trust or a decedent's estate.

Counterterrorism Data. Reveal uses counterterrorism data from various sources on individuals.

Outputs

Reveal's outputs include reports that contain names, Social Security numbers, addresses, and other personal identifiers of individuals suspected of financial crimes, including corporate and tax fraud, and of terrorist activity. Reports are shared with IRS agents who conduct investigations based on the report's results.

FBI's Foreign Terrorist Tracking Task Force Data Mining Effort

The data mining effort used by the Federal Bureau of Investigation's (FBI) Foreign Terrorist Tracking Task Force analyzes intelligence and detects terrorist activities. In support of its responsibilities, the task force operates two information systems—one unclassified and one classified—that form the basis of its data mining activities.

Purpose and Uses

The purpose of the task force's data mining effort is to analyze intelligence and detect terrorist activities.[1] The task force supports ongoing investigations in law enforcement agencies and the intelligence community by using its data mining effort to respond to requests for information about foreign terrorists from FBI agents or officials from a partner agency.[2] For example, task force program officials informed us that they occasionally receive information about specific threats from the intelligence community or law enforcement partners. When such threat information is received, they identify potential sources of information that may reveal persons capable and motivated to carry out the threat. They then connect this information with persons listed in other databases linked to terrorist information. The task force then provides the names of high risk individuals whose characteristics match the threat profile to FBI field agencies and to Joint Terrorist Task Force(s).

According to task force officials, analysts conduct research and analysis based on requests and provide a report of the results to the requesters and to affected agencies, as appropriate. For example, according to agency officials, the task force received a list of possible suicide bombers from a foreign government. Through analysis, the task force determined that several of the bombers had names and other identifiers that were similar to those of individuals currently in the United States. The task force provided the information to law enforcement investigators to determine whether the individuals identified were the same as those on the list of suicide bombers provided by the foreign government.

---

[1]The task force's mission is to assist federal law enforcement and intelligence agencies in locating foreign terrorists and their supporters who are in or have visited the United States, and to provide information to other law enforcement and intelligence community agencies that can lead to their surveillance, prosecution, or removal.

[2]The task force's partner agencies include Immigration and Customs Enforcement, the Department of Defense Counterintelligence Field Activity office, the Office of Personnel Management, and members of the intelligence community.

How It Works

Task force analysts use two systems together in their data mining effort: one sensitive but unclassified, and one classified. After receiving a request for information about a threat or person of interest, task force leadership routes the information to an appropriate analyst. Analysts initially search within the task force's existing data, including certain immigration records, to determine whether they already have information relevant to the request.

Task force analysts use several analytical tools to help search for and analyze information in the systems. According to task force officials, the analysts' primary query tool is the Query Tracking and Initiation Program. FBI developed this program to allow users to search the systems using, among other things, multiple variants or transliterations of names. It also allows analysts to search within and between different data sets.

The unclassified system serves as the initial repository for unclassified data. Through this system, task force analysts can use the query tracking program to submit queries on individuals to commercial databases to find any relevant information. The resulting information is returned to the unclassified system, where analysts can conduct analysis using query tracking and other tools.

The classified system contains law enforcement and intelligence data, including FBI case files. Information initially collated in the unclassified system is loaded into the classified system daily. However, if analysts need expedited results, they can perform an initial analysis using data contained in the unclassified system and then conduct a more detailed analysis once data are loaded into the classified system. The two systems are illustrated in figure 5.

Figure 5: An Overview of FBI's Foreign Terrorist Tracking Task Force Data Mining Effort

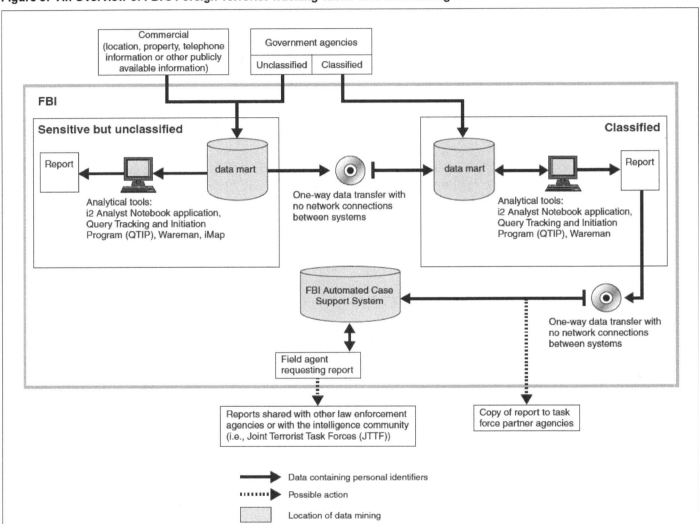

Source: GAO analysis of agency data.

Inputs

FBI officials reported that the task force's systems contain multiple sets of data from multiple government and nongovernment sources, some of which were acquired on a one-time basis and others that are regularly updated. Data from outside sources, including nonpartner government agencies and commercial entities, are typically acquired on an as-needed basis.

Government Data from Systems of Records

Twenty-nine of the task force's government data sets are part of a system of records. Many of these data sets come from within the Department of Justice. Other agencies also supply the task force with data, including information from immigration records, from the Federal Aviation Administration, and from Customs and Border Protection. According to program officials, most data that come from sources outside the Department of Justice are acquired under a provision of the Privacy Act that allows a law enforcement agency to request certain data from a government entity for law enforcement purposes. According to agency officials, outside agencies provided their data sets to FBI on the basis of formal requests.

Government Data Not from Systems of Records

The task force's data mining effort receives one set of government data that is not part of a system of records because the information does not contain personal identifiers.

The task force data mining system also contains 15 data sets that include information on criminal aliens, intelligence data and alerts, and various watchlists. FBI officials responsible for the task force were unaware of whether these data are part of a system of records, but said that the data were supplied to the task force under the same conditions as other government data.

Commercial Data

The task force data mining effort uses data from several commercial sources,[3] many of which are updated frequently. According to FBI officials, analysts can query commercial sources during the course of an investigation, if needed. Program officials noted that analysts request information from commercial sources using personal identifiers.

Data from International Entities

The task force received 4 data sets from Interpol (an international police organization) on wanted persons, stolen property and other intelligence.

---

[3]Commercial data are maintained by private companies and can include personally identifiable information that either identifies an individual or is directly attributed to an individual, such as name, address, and telephone number.

Outputs

The task force's outputs include reports that contain personal identifiers and other information that is relevant to the initial request. Reports are shared with the requesting entity or agent and as needed with partner agencies. Agents conduct investigations based on the results of the reports.

Small Business Administration's Loan/Lender Monitoring System

The Small Business Administration (SBA) contracted with Dun & Bradstreet to provide information and analytical capabilities that assist SBA in managing credit risks in two major business loan guarantee programs. The Loan/Lender Monitoring System (L/LMS) combines SBA data with private sector data on businesses and consumers to predict future performance of outstanding business loans.

Purpose and Uses

The purpose of L/LMS is to identify, measure, and manage risk in two of its business loan programs. It does this specifically by developing predictive ratings that allow SBA to improve the performance of two of its business loan programs—the 7(a) loan program[1] and 504 program[2]—using risk management principles. The system analyzes SBA loan data, Dun & Bradstreet business data, and data provided by subcontractors, including consumer credit bureau information and business credit scores. It uses a commercially available suite of scorecards to produce business credit scores that predict the likelihood of an SBA loan becoming severely delinquent over the next 18 to 24 months—a leading indicator of default.[3] It also contains trends databases that provide historical data on approximately one dozen performance and credit risk fields on each outstanding loan.

Finally, the system contains lender databases that provide information about individual lenders that can be compared to the information about a lender's peers.

---

[1]Under the 7(a) loan program, SBA can provide guarantees on loans made by participating lenders authorized by SBA. The 7(a) program is intended for small business borrowers who could not otherwise obtain credit under suitable terms and conditions from the private sector without an SBA guarantee. SBA guarantees approximately $14 to $16 billion lender-originated 7(a) loans each year, of which SBA guarantees only approximately $9 to $10 billion each year. Upon default by a borrower, the participating lender may request that SBA purchase the guaranteed portion of a loan.

[2]The 504 program provides long-term, fixed-rate financing to small businesses for expansion or modernization, primarily for real estate and major assets such as heavy equipment. The 504 financing is delivered through nonprofit corporations established to contribute to the economic development of their communities. SBA guarantees about $4 billion in 504 loans annually.

[3]A loan is severely delinquent when payments on the loan are past due by 60 or more days.

How it Works	Dun & Bradstreet and Fair Isaac use the input data in a proprietary scoring process to generate a predictive risk score for each outstanding loan. In addition, Dun & Bradstreet appends its commercial demographic and risk data to the electronic records of all outstanding SBA business loans, after removing any personal identifiers. Dun & Bradstreet then transfers this information to a module where it can be accessed by SBA. None of the data transferred from Dun & Bradstreet to SBA contains personal identifiers.

SBA can use the L/LMS to view its entire business loan or lender portfolio and can perform analysis by various data elements, including dollars outstanding, lender, lender corporate family, SBA region, industry sector, and loan type. According to SBA officials, the agency uses system-produced reports to help them determine which lenders' SBA business loan portfolios are most at risk of default, driving the selection of lenders for further review. Figure 6 depicts this process.

Inputs	The L/LMS uses two kinds of input data: data from government systems of records and data from commercial sources. The data include information on businesses and individuals.
Government Data from Systems of Records	*SBA Loan Records.* SBA electronically transfers about 10 data files monthly to Dun & Bradstreet. These files contain existing data on individual 7(a) and 504 SBA business loans and on the lending institutions that manage the loans and include information on small businesses; names, addresses, and phone numbers, as well as limited information about business principals, including personal identifiers.

Figure 6: An Overview of the Loan/Lender Monitoring System

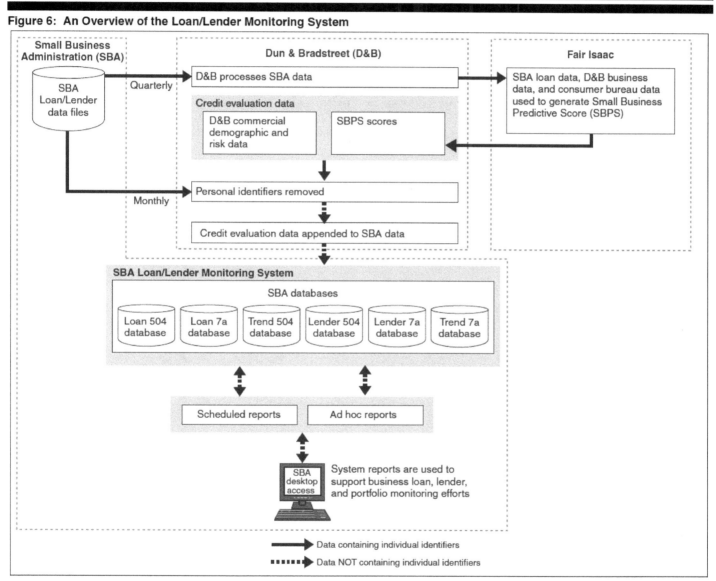

Source: GAO analysis of agency data.

Commercial Data

Credit Evaluation Data. The L/LMS uses several sources of commercial data, including Dun & Bradstreet demographic and risk data from its global business database, consumer bureau data on the business principals (e.g., information relating to recent delinquencies), and predictive risk scores developed by Dun & Bradstreet and Fair Isaac.[4] This information can contain personal identifiers.

Outputs

The L/LMS analyzes the data to generate reports on each lender's portfolio. SBA also creates aggregate reports that evaluate loans by portfolio value, projected risk, and historical performance trends. According to SBA officials, system reports are currently used by program officials to support business loan, lender, and portfolio monitoring efforts.

---

[4]Fair Isaac is a company that provides business and consumer analytical services, including credit ratings.

Detailed Assessments of Agency Actions to Address Security Requirements in Data Mining Efforts

The Privacy Act requires agencies to establish appropriate administrative, technical, and physical safeguards to ensure the security of records and to protect against any anticipated threats or hazards to their security that could result in substantial harm, embarrassment, inconvenience, or unfairness to any individual about whom information is maintained. Although the act does not specify the procedures agencies should employ to ensure information security, subsequent legislation and guidance from the Office of Management and Budget (OMB) and the National Institute of Standards and Technology (NIST) provide specific procedures that agencies should take to protect the security of information.

For example, the Federal Information Security Management Act (FISMA) requires that agencywide information security programs include detailed plans for providing adequate information security for networks, facilities, and systems or groups of information systems, as appropriate. OMB requires that agencies prepare IT system security plans consistent with NIST guidance, and that these plans contain specific elements, including rules of behavior for system use, required training in security responsibilities, personnel controls, technical security techniques and controls, continuity of operations, incident response, and system interconnection.[1] In addition, OMB requires that agency management officials formally authorize their information systems to process information and thereby accept the risk associated with their operation. This management authorization (accreditation) is to be supported by a formal technical evaluation (certification) of the management, operational, and technical controls established in an information system's security plan. NIST guidelines detail the requirements for certification and accreditation, including the requirement that the certification documents include the system security plan, risk assessment, and tested contingency plan.[2] In addition, NIST guidance on recommended security controls for federal information systems requires agencies to develop, implement, and test contingency plans for their systems and risk assessments.

---

[1]NIST, *The Security Certification and Accreditation of Federal Information Systems*, Special Publication 800-37 (May 2004) and Office of Management and Budget, Management of Federal Information Resources, Circular No. A-130, Revised, Transmittal Memorandum No. 4, Appendix III, "Security of Federal Automated Information Resources" (Nov. 28, 2000).

[2]NIST, *Guide for the Security Certification and Accreditation of Federal Information Systems*, Special Publication 800-37 (May 2004).

Table 10 lists each of the security requirements that we evaluated and the results of our evaluation for each of the five data mining efforts included in this report.

Table 10: Questions Related to Agency Actions Safeguarding and Ensuring the Quality of Records Containing Personal Information

Question	Yes	Partial	No	Exempt
Has the agency performed a risk assessment to determine the information system vulnerabilities, identify threats, and develop countermeasures to those threats?	ACDE		B	
Has the agency developed a security plan for each system?	CD	AE	B	
Does the plan address—				
rules of the system?	ACDE		B	
training?	ACDE		B	
personnel controls?	ACDE		B	
incident response capability?	CD	AE	B	
system interconnection?	ACDE		B	
Has the agency had the system certified and accredited by management?	ADE		B	C[a]
Did the certification documentation include an approval document including a statement of risk acceptance?	ADE		B	C[a]
Has the agency performed testing and evaluation of the data-mining system(s)?	DE	AC[a]	B	
Was the testing and evaluation—				
conducted no less than annually?	DE	AC[a]	B	
conducted using NIST Special Publication 800-26 or appropriate alternative?	DE	A	BC	
conducted using an element of internal penetration or vulnerability testing?	CDE		AB	
Does the agency have a tested contingency plan for the system?	CE	AD	B	
Did the agency take steps to ensure the accuracy, relevance, timeliness, and completeness of the data it maintains?	B	E	A	CD

Legend:

A: RMA's data mining effort

B: State's Citibank Custom Reporting System

C: IRS's Reveal effort

D: FBI's Foreign Terrorist Tracking Task Force effort

E: SBA's Lender/Loan Monitoring System

Source: GAO analysis of agency information.

[a]The IRS Reveal effort became operational in February 2005 and has interim authority to operate—not full certification and accreditation. IRS is currently testing the system.

Comments from the U.S. Department of Agriculture

United States Department of Agriculture

Risk Management Agency

1400 Independence Avenue, SW Stop 0806 Washington, DC 20250-0806

Ms. Linda Koontz
Director, Information Management
Government Accountability Office
441 G Street, NW Rm. 4075
Washington, DC 20548

JUL 2 2 2005

Dear Ms. Koontz:

Attached is the Risk Management Agency's (RMA) response to your draft report titled, "Data Mining: Agencies Have Taken Key Steps to Protect Privacy in Selected Efforts, but Significant Compliance Issues Remain." In addition to the attached written response, RMA also provided technical comments to GAO via email. RMA appreciates the opportunity to provide comments. If you have any questions regarding our response, please contact Heather Manzano at 202-690-5886.

Sincerely,

Ross J. Davidson, Jr.
Administrator
Risk Management Agency

Attachment

The Risk Management Agency Administers
And Oversees All Programs Authorized Under
The Federal Crop Insurance Corporation

An Equal Opportunity Employer

U.S. Department of Agriculture
Statement of Action on the
U.S. Government Accountability Office Draft Report GAO-05-866
"DATA MINING: Agencies Have Taken Key Steps to Protect Privacy in Selected Efforts, but
Significant Compliance Issues Remain"

July 22, 2005

Data mining is an effort that is being used increasingly by the federal government. This effort
involves the use of personal information, which can originate from various sources. GAO was
asked to describe the characteristics of five federal data mining efforts and to determine whether
agencies are providing adequate privacy and security protection for the information systems and
the individuals potentially affected by these data mining efforts.

As a result of the study, GAO developed six recommendations for the United States Department
of Agriculture (USDA) specific to the Risk Management Agency (RMA). The following
addresses those recommendations.

GAO Recommendation 1

Provide the required Privacy Act notices to individuals, including producers, insurance agents,
and adjusters, when personal information is collected from them.

USDA Response

RMA will issue an Informational Memorandum to private insurance companies who deliver the
Federal crop insurance program to ensure they are aware of their responsibilities regarding
notification at the point of personal information data collection, as required in the Privacy Act.

GAO Recommendation 2

Apply the appropriate information security measures defined in OMB and NIST guidance to the
systems used in the RMA data mining effort, including the development of a system security
plan, a tested contingency plan, and regular testing and evaluation of the systems used in this
effort.

USDA Response

RMA has applied the appropriate information security measures defined in OMB and NIST
guidance to the systems used in the RMA data mining effort. This project has a system security
plan, and RMA performs regular testing and evaluation of the system. RMA will be testing their
existing data mining contingency plan before the end of the year.

GAO Recommendation 3

Develop and implement procedures that ensure the accuracy, relevance, timeliness, and completeness of personal information used in the RMA data mining effort to make determinations about individuals.

USDA Response

RMA has procedures in place to ensure accuracy of information used in the data mining effort. RMA performs a series of edits and validations on data submitted by the insurance companies. Accepted data is then sent to the Data Warehouse on a monthly basis. This data is used in various scenario analyses. Reports are generated from these analyses and are provided to RMA for review and action in accordance with procedures. Any data observations that appear anomalous through the data mining effort, are reviewed by RMA prior to a report being issued. If appropriate, RMA may make changes to the edit/validation process based on these observations. The goal of this data review process is to clarify and, if possible, resolve any data discrepancies prior to generating a report.

GAO Recommendation 4

Revise the privacy impact assessment for the RMA data mining effort to comply with OMB guidance, including analyses of the intended use of the information it collects, with whom the information will be shared, how the information is to be secured, opportunities for impacted individuals to comment, and the choices made by the agency as a result of the assessment.

USDA Response

RMA is finalizing the template that will be used for all of its privacy impact analyses (PIA). All new PIAs and updated reviews will utilize this new format.

GAO Recommendation 5

Have the completed privacy impact assessment approved by the Chief Information Officer or equivalent official.

USDA Response

As in the past, the RMA Chief Information Officer and his designated reviewers will evaluate and review the completed PIAs. The new PIA format requires the signatures of the CIO, Freedom of Information Act (FOIA) Officer, system owner, and project manager.

GAO Recommendation 6

Make the completed privacy impact assessment available to the public, as appropriate.

<u>USDA Response</u>

The RMA CIO, in cooperation with the FOIA Officer, will make the PIAs available to the public, as appropriate.

<u>General Comments</u>

RMA agrees with the majority of GAO's recommendations and believes that the agency has taken steps to put many of those recommendations into action. However, RMA does not agree with the numerous statements that indicate that the agency did not take steps to ensure the accuracy, relevance, timeliness, and completeness of the data it maintains and uses to make determinations about individuals. Program officials *are* aware of the need to ensure the quality of data, and RMA's upfront edit and validation *does* provide reasonable assurance of the accuracy and adequacy of the data prior to sending it to the data warehouse.

In addition, RMA respectfully disagrees with GAO's assessment that RMA has only partially achieved the completion of a plan that addresses incident response capability. During the on-site review, GAO was provided a copy of RMA's policy that addresses this subject. It was also addressed in the data mining system security plan.

Comments from the Department of the Treasury

DEPARTMENT OF THE TREASURY
WASHINGTON, D.C. 20220

JUL 29 2005

Ms. Linda D. Koontz
Director, Information Management
Government Accountability Office
Washington, DC

Dear Ms. Koontz:

Thank you for the opportunity to review Government Accountability Office (GAO) Draft Report GAO-05-866, *Data Mining: Agencies Have Taken Steps to Protect Privacy in Selected Efforts, but Significant Compliance Issues Remain.* The Department's response to the specific recommendations made in the Report to the Secretary of the Treasury follows:

Recommendation 1: Apply the appropriate information security measures defined in the Office of Management and Budget (OMB) and the National Institute of Standards and Technology (NIST) guidance to the systems used in the Reveal data mining effort:

The Department of the Treasury's Internal Revenue Service (IRS) security procedures are in compliance with OMB, NIST, and Treasury guidance. Reveal is a Commercial Off-the-Shelf (COTS) software product and is a pilot system which resides on the Criminal Investigation infrastructure or System Domain General Support System (GSS). For the Reveal System, IRS granted an Interim Authorization to Operate (IATO), following the guidance outlined in the NIST 800-37, Guide for the Security Certification and Accreditation of Federal Information Systems. In addition, IRS granted an IATO for the infrastructure which is currently in the accreditation phase of the NIST compliant Certification & Accreditation (C&A) process.

Recommendation 2: Revise the privacy impact assessment for the IRS Reveal system to comply with OMB guidance, including analyses of the information to be collected, the purposes of the collection, the intended use of the information, how the information is to be secured, and opportunities for impacted individuals to comment.

Since the Reveal system is in pilot, a new PIA is required by IRS policy before launching the system into full deployment. At that time, the IRS will assess and document changes or modifications to the system as a combination of the pilot results, the PIA, and the security reviews and certification. Prior to conducting this new PIA, the IRS will be revising the current PIA to incorporate all OMB guidance, in particular adding the question of what choices were made as a result of conducting the PIA.

However, it is also important to note that the IRS PIA is far more comprehensive in its questions and assessments than the OMB guidance. Since 1995, the IRS has been completing PIA for its systems. The IRS PIA is more comprehensive in its questions and assessments than the OMB guidance (19 questions compared with 8 on the OMB PIA).

1

Finally, we refer you to the IRS Reveal PIA question 15 which describes and analyzes why the information was collected, the purpose of the collection, and the intended use of the information. Reveal is an IRS Criminal Investigation Division analytical application that provides users with an enhanced capability to access, analyze, and interpret large volumes of disparate data sources, through a single-point of access, for the purpose of identifying and developing criminal cases. The system is used to identify potential criminal investigations of individuals or groups in support of the overall IRS Mission. Reveal supports the Criminal Investigation mission by identifying persons or organizations involved in potential criminal violations of the Internal Revenue Code and related financial crimes in a manner that fosters confidence in the tax system and compliance with the law.

We also direct you to the IRS PIA questions 8 through 13 in response to how the information was secured. These questions established a strong framework of administrative and technical controls. In addition, the IRS PIA is an integral component of the security certification of all new IRS systems.

Recommendation 3: Make the completed privacy impact assessment available to the public, as appropriate.

The current Reveal PIA is available on the IRS Website. Revisions to the PIA will be posted to the public website as well.

Sincerely,

Ira L. Hobbs
Chief Information Officer

2

Comments from the Department of State

United States Department of State

Assistant Secretary and Chief Financial Officer

Washington, D.C. 20520

Ms. Jacquelyn Williams-Bridgers
Managing Director
International Affairs and Trade
Government Accountability Office
441 G Street, N.W.
Washington, D.C. 20548-0001

. JUL 2 5 2005

Dear Ms. Williams-Bridgers:

We appreciate the opportunity to review your draft report, "DATA MINING: Agencies Have Taken Key Steps to Protect Privacy in Selected Efforts, but Significant Compliance Issues Remain," GAO Job Code 310715.

The enclosed Department of State comments are provided for incorporation with this letter as an appendix to the final report.

If you have any questions concerning this response, please contact Margaret Colaianni, Procurement Analyst, Bureau of Administration, at (202) 736-4985.

Sincerely,

Sid Kaplan (Acting)

cc: GAO – Marcia Washington
      A – Frank Coulter
      State/OIG – Mark Duda

Department of State Comments on GAO Draft Report
<u>Data Mining: Agencies Have Taken Key Steps to Protect Privacy in</u>
<u>Selected Efforts, but Significant Compliance Issues Remain</u>
(GAO-05-866, GAO Code 310715)

I. <u>Introduction</u>

Thank you for allowing us to comment on your draft report entitled, "Data Mining: Agencies Have Taken Key Steps to Protect Privacy in Selected Efforts, but Significant Compliance Issues Remain". We have responded below to the single recommendation to State. In addition, we have also recommended some changes to the text of the draft report (highlighted in bold with italics) that we believe will enhance the consistency between the report and its recommendations.

We appreciate that you have not recommended that the Department conduct a Privacy Impact Assessment with respect to the Citibank purchase card system. As your report points out, OMB's E-Gov implementing guidelines specify that agencies need not prepare Privacy Impact Assessments for systems "where information relates to internal government operations." (Similarly, the OMB guidelines clarify that Privacy Impact Assessments are required *only* when an agency is (a) "developing or procuring IT systems . . . that collect, maintain or disseminate information in identifiable form *about members of the public*" or (b) collecting information "for 10 or more persons *excluding . . . employees of the federal government* . . . ." (Emphasis added.)) Many of our recommended changes reflect our efforts to clarify that the Department is not required to conduct a Privacy Impact Assessment of the Citibank system.

We also appreciate that you have not made any recommendations about the Department's compliance with the Federal Information Security Management Act of 2002 (FISMA) vis-à-vis the Citibank purchase card. It is not clear that FISMA necessarily applies to the Citibank system.

II. <u>Department of State action in response to GAO recommendation</u>

<u>Notify purchase card participants of the legal basis under which the Department collects their personal information, as required</u>. In response to this recommendation, the Department of State will take the necessary steps to notify purchase card participants of the legal basis under which the Department collects their personal information necessary for the operation and management of our worldwide Purchase Card program.

- 2 -

Comments from the Small Business Administration

U.S. SMALL BUSINESS ADMINISTRATION
WASHINGTON, D.C. 20416

Linda D. Koontz
Director
Information Management Issues
U.S. Government Accountability Office
Washington, DC 20548-0001

Dear Ms. Koontz:

Thank you for the opportunity to review and comment on the Government Accountability Office's (GAO) draft report on *Data Mining: Agencies Have Taken Key Steps to Protect Privacy in Selected Efforts, but Significant Compliance Issues Remain* (GAO-05-866). We appreciate GAO's acknowledgement that the U.S. Small Business Administration (SBA) has substantially complied with existing guidance and regulatory requirements governing privacy and information security in operating our Loan and Lender Monitoring System.

With regard to the three recommendations contained in the draft report, SBA provides the following response:

1. GAO Recommendation: Amend the system of records notice regarding its data mining effort to clearly identify the individual responsible for the effort, the process by which individuals can request notification that the system includes records about them, and the procedures individuals should use to review records pertaining to them.

    SBA Response: SBA believes the Agency System of Records is comprehensive but will review the system of records for the Loan System to determine if clarifications are necessary.

2. GAO Recommendation: Complete a privacy impact assessment for the data *mining effort that complies with OMB guidance, including analyses of the information to be collected, the purposes of the collection, the intended use of the information, how the information is to be secured, opportunities for impacted individuals to comment, and the choices made by the agency as a result of the assessment.

    SBA Response: As noted in the draft report, SBA plans to issue a revised privacy impact assessment (PIA) for the Loan and Lender Monitoring System later this fiscal year that will address GAO's recommendation.

SBA IS AN EQUAL OPPORTUNITY EMPLOYER AND PROVIDER

Federal Recycling Program   Printed on Recycled Paper

3. **GAO Recommendation:** Make the completed privacy impact assessment available to the public, as appropriate.

SBA Response: As with the current PIA for SBA's Loan and Lender Monitoring System, the revised assessment will be available to the public, as appropriate.

In addition, certain factual clarifications were identified. They are summarized in the enclosure with this letter.

We appreciate the opportunity to work with your staff during the conduct of this audit. Should you have any questions, please contact C. Edward Rowe, Assistant Administrator for Congressional and Legislative Affairs at (202) 205-6700.

Sincerely,

Michael W. Hager
Associate Deputy Administrator
for Office of Capital Access

Enclosure

GAO Contact and Staff Acknowledgments

GAO Contact

Linda D. Koontz (202) 512-6240

Acknowledgments

In addition to the contact named above, Barbara Collier, Neil Doherty, Mirko Dolak, Nancy Glover, Alison Jacobs, Kathleen S. Lovett, David Plocher, James R. Sweetman, Jr., and Marcia Washington made key contributions to this report.